STATE CAPACITY AND ECONOMIC DEVELOPMENT

Present and Past

Mark Dincecco
University of Michigan

POLITICAL ECONOMY

David Stavasage

CAMBRIDGE
UNIVERSITY PRESS

Cambridge Elements ☰

CAMBRIDGE
UNIVERSITY PRESS

University Printing House, Cambridge CB2 8BS, United Kingdom

One Liberty Plaza, 20th Floor, New York, NY 10006, USA

477 Williamstown Road, Port Melbourne, VIC 3207, Australia

4843/24, 2nd Floor, Ansari Road, Daryaganj, Delhi – 110002, India

79 Anson Road, #06–04/06, Singapore 079906

Cambridge University Press is part of the University of Cambridge.

It furthers the University's mission by disseminating knowledge in the pursuit of education, learning, and research at the highest international levels of excellence.

www.cambridge.org
Information on this title: www.cambridge.org/9781108439541
DOI: 10.1017/9781108539913

© Mark Dincecco 2017

First published 2017

A catalogue record for this publication is available from the British Library.

ISBN 978-1-108-43954-1 Paperback
ISSN 2398-4031 (Online)
ISSN 2514-3816 (Print)

State Capacity and Economic Development

Mark Dincecco

Abstract *State capacity – the government's ability to accomplish its intended policy goals – plays an important role in market-oriented economic development today. Yet state capacity improvements are often difficult to achieve. To better understand this puzzle, this inquiry analyzes the historical origins of state capacity. I evaluate long-run state development in Western Europe – the birthplace of both the modern state and modern economic growth – with a focus on three key inflection points: the rise of the city-state, the rise of the nation-state, and the rise of the welfare state. To guide this analysis, I develop a conceptual framework regarding the basic political conditions that enable the state to take effective policy actions. This framework highlights the government's challenge to exert proper authority over both its citizenry and itself. I conclude this inquiry by analyzing the European state development process relative to other world regions. This analysis characterizes the basic historical features that helped make Western Europe different. Overall, by taking a long-run approach, this inquiry provides a new perspective on the deep-rooted relationship between state capacity and economic development.*

Keywords: *state capacity, effective governance, rules of the game, economic development, historical analysis, Europe, city-state, nation-state, welfare state, comparative perspective, China, sub-Saharan Africa*

ISSNs: 2398-4031 (Online), 2514-3816 (Print)
ISBNs: 9781108539913 PB, 9781108439541 OC

I greatly thank David Stasavage and an anonymous referee for numerous helpful comments during the development of this manuscript. In 2016–17, I was the

1 State Capacity and Economic Development Today

The Northern Triangle nations – El Salvador, Guatemala, and Honduras – are among the most violent in the world. The homicide rates in both El Salvador and Guatemala were roughly 40 murders per 100,000 people in 2012, while in Honduras the homicide rate was 90 (United Nations, 2014: 126). Such high homicide rates were 7 to 15 times greater than the global average homicide rate in this year (United Nations, 2014: 12). In the Northern Triangle, therefore, governments fail to perform their most basic duty: the protection of life. Police, prosecutors, and judges in Guatemala, for example, are severely understaffed (*Economist*, 2006). Similarly, police corruption in Honduras is rampant: more than 95 percent of homicides in recent years did not result in conviction (*New York Times*, 2016; Reuters, 2016). The state's inability to provide basic security in the Northern Triangle impedes economic development, since fearful individuals must think twice before partaking in the sorts of market commerce and private investments that characterize a vibrant economy.

The problem of weak state performance extends far beyond the Northern Triangle. The national government in Afghanistan (South Asia), for example, cannot properly secure its main commercial highway (*New York Times*, 2014). Travelers must guard against ambush, hidden explosives, and sniper fire. High threats of violence raise the cost of trade to and from the capital city of Kabul, hindering economic activity. Meanwhile, wood charcoal burners in Malawi (sub-Saharan Africa) have cut down too many forest trees, making it difficult for the forest floor to absorb water during the

Edward Teller National Fellow at the Hoover Institution at Stanford University. This manuscript was written during my time there. I offer special thanks to Director Thomas Gilligan and Senior Fellows Stephen Haber and Jonathan Rodden for facilitating this wonderful research opportunity. I am likewise very grateful to the Department of Political Science at the University of Michigan, my beloved home institution, for generous research support over the past several years. Finally, I kindly thank Thomas Baunsgaard, Michael Keen, and David Stasavage for data-sharing.

rainy season and gradually yield it throughout the year (*New York Times*, 2016). Deforestation has created both water shortages and power blackouts (by undercutting the supply of hydroelectricity) in the capital city of Lilongwe, stifling economic productivity.

Poor state performance is not always as extreme as in the examples described above. Governments in many developing nations today are able to fulfill at least some core state functions. Nonetheless, what often binds weakly performing governments – whether in acute cases such as Somalia or relatively moderate cases such as Peru – is a similar underlying problem: the lack of adequate state capacity.

By "state capacity," I mean the state's ability to accomplish its intended policy actions – economic, fiscal, and otherwise. This conceptualization corresponds with Mann's (1986) classic notion of the infrastructural power of the state. Mann (1986: 113) writes: "We might term this 'infrastructural power,' the capacity of the state actually to penetrate civil society, and to implement logistically political decisions throughout the realm."

The remainder of this section performs three main tasks. First, I offer stylized evidence about the relationship between state capacity and economic development today. Next, I discuss different channels through which greater state capacity may in fact improve growth prospects. Finally, I draw on both types of material to motivate my subsequent analysis of the historical origins of state capacity.

1.1 Stylized Evidence

Figure 1 offers a first systematic look at the state's potential economic role. There is a strong positive correlation between the tax/GDP ratio – a raw measure of the extractive capacity of the state – and per capita GDP across 140-plus modern-day nations. Wealthy nations in world regions including Western Europe and North America gather higher tax revenue as a share of GDP than poor nations in parts of Africa, Asia, and Latin America.

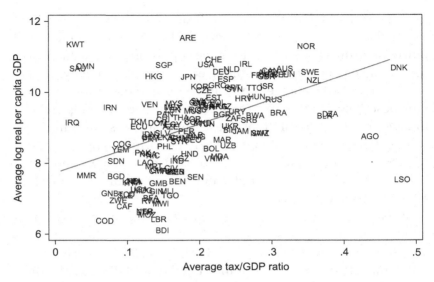

Figure 1 Total Taxation and GDP Today
Notes: Log real per capita GDP is in constant 2011 national prices
(in millions of 2011 US dollars). Tax/GDP ratio is the ratio of total
tax revenue to GDP. Data are averaged over 2000–9. Nations with
populations of less than one million in 2000 are excluded.
Sources: Feenstra, Inklaar, and Timmer (2015) for GDP and the
IMF World Revenue Longitudinal Database for tax/GDP ratio.

Figure 2 replaces the tax/GDP ratio with the income tax/total tax
ratio. The collection of income tax revenue requires high administrative capacity to enforce compliance (Besley and Persson, 2013:
54, 56–7). Thus, the share of income tax revenue in total tax
revenue is an important measure of the state's fiscal prowess.
There is a strong positive relationship between the income tax
share and per capita GDP.

For a different perspective, Figure 3 plots the correlation
between the state weakness score according to Rice and Patrick
(2008) and log per capita GDP in the developing world today. This
relationship is downward-sloping: as the state becomes weaker,
per capita GDP declines. This evidence suggests that the state's

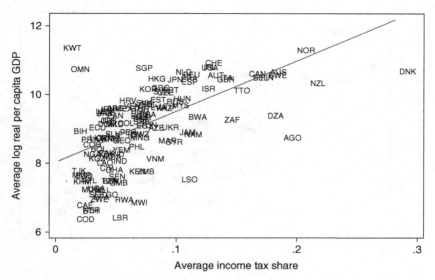

Figure 2 Income Taxation and GDP Today
Notes: Log real per capita GDP is in constant 2011 national prices (in millions of 2011 US dollars). Income tax share is the ratio of income tax revenue to total tax revenue. Data are averaged over 2000–9. Nations with populations of less than one million in 2000 are excluded.
Sources: Feenstra, Inklaar, and Timmer (2015) for GDP and the IMF World Revenue Longitudinal Database for tax/GDP ratio.

lack of ability to accomplish basic governance tasks may reduce development prospects.

The stylized evidence above suggests that greater state capacity can facilitate economic development. We must be careful, however, not to mistake correlation with causation. Put differently, the correct causal logic may run from economic development to state capacity improvements, and not the other way around. I will return to this topic throughout this inquiry, arguing that there are ample reasons to think – particularly over the long stretch of history – that the main direction of causation runs from greater state capacity to economic development, and not vice versa.

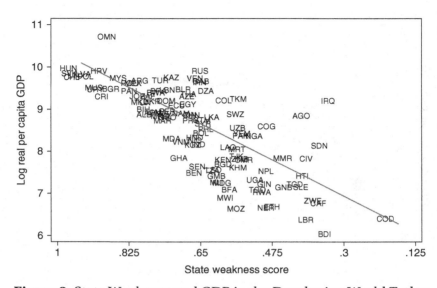

Figure 3 State Weakness and GDP in the Developing World Today
Notes: Log real per capita GDP in 2006 is in constant 2011
national prices (in millions of 2011 US dollars). State weakness
refers to overall state weakness on a normalized 0–1 scale in 2006,
whereby a 0 score is the most weak and a 1 score is the least weak.
Rice and Patrick (2008: 3) measure overall state weakness in terms
of the state's ability to accomplish the following four tasks:
"fostering an environment conducive to sustainable and equitable
economic growth; establishing and maintaining legitimate,
transparent, and accountable political institutions; securing their
populations from violent conflict and controlling their territory;
and meeting the basic human needs of their population." Nations
with populations of less than one million in 2006 are excluded.
Sources: Feenstra, Inklaar, and Timmer (2015) for GDP and Rice
and Patrick (2008) for state weakness score (as reported by Besley
and Persson, 2011).

The above evidence, however, does not imply that government is the solution to each and every economic problem.
On the contrary, I will argue in Section 2 that clear limits to
state power can improve economic performance. To illustrate

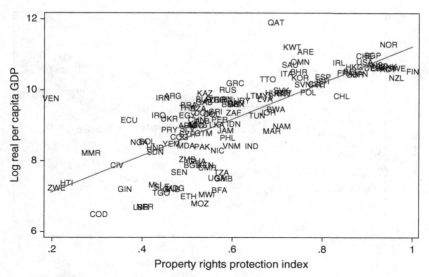

Figure 4 Property Rights Protection and GDP Today
Notes: Log real per capita GDP in 2010 is in constant 2011 national prices (in millions of 2011 US dollars). Property rights protection refers to the extent of government anti-diversion efforts on a normalized 0–1 scale in 2010, whereby 0 is the weakest such efforts and 1 is the strongest such efforts. Drawing on Besley and Persson (2011: codebook, 6), I computed government anti-diversion efforts as the average over four components from the International Country Risk Guide: law and order, bureaucratic quality, corruption, and investment risk. Nations with populations of less than one million in 2010 are excluded.
Sources: Feenstra, Inklaar, and Timmer (2015) for GDP and the International Country Risk Guide for property rights protection index.

this point, Figure 4 plots property rights protection against per capita GDP. There is a strong positive correlation between the extent to which the state respects private investment incentives – through law and order, bureaucratic quality, low corruption, and low investment risk – and modern-day economic development.

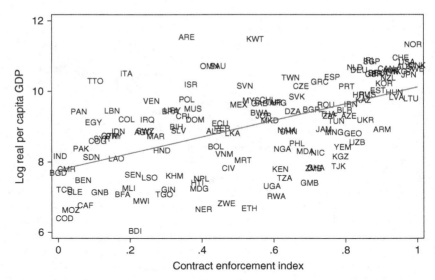

Figure 5 Contract Enforcement and GDP Today
Notes: Log real per capita GDP in 2006 is in constant 2011
national prices (in millions of 2011 US dollars). Contract
enforcement refers to the nation's relative rank in contract
enforcement on a normalized 0–1 scale in 2006, whereby 0 is the
lowest such enforcement and 1 is the highest such enforcement.
Nations with populations of less than one million in 2006 are
excluded.
Sources: Feenstra, Inklaar, and Timmer (2015) for GDP and the
World Bank Doing Business Database for contract enforcement
index (as reported by Besley and Persson, 2011).

Similarly, there is a strong positive relationship between contract enforcement by the state and per capita GDP today
(Figure 5). Finally, tax revenue tends to be higher for political
regimes that place institutional checks on executive power
(Acemoglu, 2005: 1200–1; Besley and Persson, 2013: 61–2).
I will offer a theoretical explanation for this somewhat counter-
intuitive relationship in the next section.

1.2 Channels

The stylized evidence in the previous section suggests that the state can play a positive economic role. I now discuss several channels through which greater state capacity may in fact promote market-oriented economic development.

1.2.1 Rules of the Game

A first channel concerns the state's ability to provide three basic public goods: domestic law and order, secure private property rights, and military defense against external attack threats. Douglass North (1981: 24) calls these types of public goods the "underlying rules of the game." Each of them can promote private investments by individuals – in new machinery, greater education, and/or technological innovations, since each reduces the likelihood of expropriation, whether by banditry, a predatory state, or a hostile foreign government. The example of the Northern Triangle nations from the start of this section illustrates how the state's inability to overcome endemic violence can impede economic activity. A similar logic holds if the state is unable to limit its own predation or offer military defense against external attackers.

A related channel concerns the state's ability to provide the fair and quick resolution of legal disputes. For example, the Sixth Amendment of the US Constitution states: "In all criminal prosecutions, the accused shall enjoy the right to a speedy and public trial, by an impartial jury of the State." This type of public good enhances domestic law and order. If the police, prosecutors, and judges are under-funded and over-worked, then the integrity of the legal system will suffer. In turn, individuals will have less incentive to make private investments, which may be subject to nefarious lawsuits. Similarly, bandits may feel more leeway to commit crimes, since the likelihood of prosecution is small.

1.2.2 Market Exchange

Beyond the rules of the game, another channel concerns the state's ability to provide a competitive and free domestic market for the exchange of goods and services (Epstein, 2000: 8–9). Adam Smith (2007: 696) calls domestic trade the "most important of all branches of commerce." Local institutional fragmentation will increase domestic trade costs. Take internal customs borders, which hinder the market exchange of goods, due to both the costs of tariff payments and the time holdups at border frontiers (Dincecco, 2011: 13–14). While we in the developed world today take competitive and free domestic markets for granted, things were not always this way. High internal tariffs, for example, created virtual autarky between regions in eighteenth-century France (Nye, 2007: 56–7).

To provide a competitive domestic market free of internal tariffs and other trade barriers (e.g., different local measures and weights), there must be a national government that is powerful enough to overcome local institutional fragmentation. Local governments themselves are unlikely to reduce trade barriers due to a pernicious free-riding problem (Olson, 1965: 1–2; Ostrom, 1990: 2–7). Namely, even if a competitive and free market would benefit the national domestic economy as a whole, each local government would prefer to free-ride on other jurisdictions by imposing tariffs on imported products from outside, while at the same time enjoying the benefit of tariff-free exports of its own products. If all local governments decide to free-ride in this way, then the domestic economy will be rife with internal customs borders, impeding overall economic performance. A national government with enough political and administrative clout, however, can overcome this free-riding problem by eliminating internal trade barriers and enforcing a competitive and free domestic market, thereby improving development prospects.

Different parts of Sections 8 to 10 of Article 1 of the US Constitution illustrate the national government's key role in resolving such free-riding. For example, Clause 1 of Section 8 states that "all duties, imposts, and excises shall be uniform throughout the United States." Similarly, Clause 5 of Section 10 states: "No state shall, without the consent of the Congress, lay any imposts or duties on imports or exports, except what may be absolutely necessary for executing its inspection laws." In such ways, the Constitution grants the national government the political authority to overcome free-riding problems related to internal trade and enforce a competitive and free domestic market.

1.2.3 Transportation Infrastructure

The state's ability to provide transportation infrastructure is yet another channel. Examples of large-scale public transportation investments include the construction of the National Trunk Highway System in China and the Interstate Highway System in the United States (Redding and Turner, 2015: 1340). Economic production depends on inputs including raw materials, labor, and fuel that may arrive from different locations (Redding and Turner, 2015: 1340). Similarly, economic consumption calls for the movement of final products to brick-and-mortar locations where consumers may buy them, or directly to the consumer's residence if bought online (Redding and Turner, 2015: 1340). By reducing the costs of moving both inputs and final products, transportation improvements can encourage domestic trade (Redding and Turner, 2015: 1361–3). Furthermore, transportation improvements can reduce commuting costs and increase the local labor supply (Redding and Turner, 2015: 1361–3). Finally, transportation infrastructure – along with public investments in communications networks (e.g., internet connectivity, postal service) – can facilitate the spread of new ideas and help spark technological innovations (Acemoglu, Moscona, and Robinson, 2016: 62). In these ways, the provision of transportation infrastruc-ture by the state can complement basic public goods including the rules of the game and a competitive and free domestic market (as described above), further improving development prospects. Beyond direct provision, moreover, the state may promote trans-portation efficiency by enforcing national standards for air, rail, and road safety and by providing incentives (e.g., fiscal) to local governments to renew their infrastructure (Glaeser, 2016). A recent review of the empirical literature by Redding and Turner (2015: 1378–83) concludes that, with few exceptions, transportation infrastructure promotes economic activity in both developed and developing nations.

1.2.4 Mass Education

A fourth channel concerns the state's ability to provide mass public education. Mass public schooling can increase the overall level of educational attainment – and thus human capital – in society (Lindert, 2004: 32). Greater human capital in turn can improve economic productivity. First, higher human capital can increase individual productivity. Higher human capital on the part of managers, moreover, can have productivity effects for firms as a whole above and beyond any individual effects (Gennaioli et al., 2013: 106). Second, greater human capital creates external effects, because workers learn from each other (Lucas, 1988: 35–9). Third, given free domestic labor mobility, workers can relocate to more productive local jurisdictions (subject to housing limits), enabling them to better exploit their human capital investments (Gennaioli et al., 2013: 107). Finally, higher levels of human capital can make technological innovations more likely (Acemoglu, Moscona, and Robinson, 2016: 61).[1] In all of these ways, public education can improve growth prospects. Gennaioli et al. (2013) construct a database that spans more than 1,500 sub-national regions across nearly 75 percent of the world's surface and nearly 100 percent of the world's GDP. They find that education levels explain a sizeable amount of regional differences in economic development.

Note that the incentive of an individual to invest in human capital in the first place depends to a great extent on the state's ability to provide the basic rules of the game as described above (i.e., law and order, private property rights, and military defense). If the state cannot provide such public goods, then the likelihood of expropriation will increase, thereby reducing the individual's

---

[1] To further promote technological innovations, the state can establish patent laws, fund research, and offer tax incentives (Acemoglu, Moscona, and Robinson, 2016: 61).

incentive to make human capital investments, regardless of the availability of public education. Similarly, if the state cannot enforce a competitive and free domestic market, then the incentive to invest in human capital will also fall, because an individual may not be able to relocate to the location where she can best take advantage of her education.

1.2.5 Social Spending

A final channel concerns the state's ability to provide social programs including housing, healthcare, retirement, unemployment compensation, and family assistance (Lindert, 2004: 6-7). The provision of such public goods by the state can be politically contentious, because they typically redistribute income from the wealthy to the poor through progressive taxation (Lindert, 2004: 6-7, 29-30).[2]

The economic effects of the social programs listed above are theoretically less straightforward than for other types of public goods. On one hand, individuals on the receiving end of social spending may respond by working fewer hours, reducing economic output (Okun, 2015: 43-44). Wealthy individuals may also decide to work less, given that social programs redistribute income away from them (Okun, 2015: 43-44). On the other hand, a social safety net can promote productive risk-taking (Benabou, 2000: 97). Furthermore, the state may help offset the potentially negative economic effects of social programs through a pro-growth and regressive tax design, well-tuned work incentives, and an open economy, which can discipline domestic producers by subjecting them to foreign competition (Lindert, 2004: 30-1).

Social spending may also have an indirect effect on economic development by reducing (net) inequality levels in society (Ostry, Berg, and Tsangarides, 2014: 9). On one hand, inequality may promote economic development, because it provides incentives

---

[2] Spending on public education is often thought to be less controversial than other social programs, in part because it is less progressive in terms of the rate at which the wealthy must transfer income to the poor (Lindert, 2004: 7).

for individuals to work hard (Lazear and Rosen, 1981: 841–2). Furthermore, inequality may enable (a subset of) individuals to overcome start-up costs and make productivity-enhancing investments in education and firms (Barro, 2000: 5–6). On the other hand, too much inequality may reduce the prospects for economic development by making mass violence and/or political revolution more likely (Alesina and Perotti, 1996: 1204). Similarly, high inequality may hinder society's ability to agree on the best policy response to negative economic shocks (Rodrik, 1999: 392–3). Finally, too much inequality may decrease the ability of poor individuals to make adequate human capital investments (Galor and Moav, 2004: 1002).

1.3 Puzzle

The discussion in Subsections 1.1 and 1.2 suggests a paradox. Greater state capacity appears to play an important role in market-oriented economic development today, but it is often difficult to achieve. To better understand this puzzle, this inquiry analyzes the historical origins of state capacity. I now justify this approach. Following Acemoglu, Johnson, and Robinson (2005: 388), we may divide the determinants of economic development into two types: proximate and fundamental. Proximate determinants concern the bread-and-butter mechanics of economic growth, including physical capital, human capital, labor force size, and total factor productivity (e.g., Solow, 1956). Yet proximate determinants are "not causes of growth; they *are* growth" (North and Thomas, 1973: 2). Which factors explain why the magnitudes of proximate variables are greater in one modern-day polity versus another? Fundamental determinants of economic development concern the basic institutions in society that structure the incentives for economic and political interactions (North and Thomas, 1973: 2–3; North, 1990: 3). To fully explain the economic growth process, we must continue to improve our knowledge of such fundamental factors. By its very nature, a proper understanding of the fundamental determinants of economic development calls for historical study. It is now well-recognized that historic events matter greatly for economic development today (Nunn, 2009: 88). In this inquiry, I analyze long-run state development in Western Europe, the birthplace of both the modern state and – not coincidentally, as I will argue – modern economic growth. By taking a historical perspective, this inquiry provides a new way to think about the "fundamentals" of the relationship between state capacity and economic development. In turn, we gain fresh insight into the process of economic growth.

My inquiry proceeds as follows. Section 2 develops a simple conceptual framework that will guide the historical analysis. Section 3 examines state development in Western Europe over the long run, with a focus on three key inflection points: the rise of the city-state, the rise of the nation-state, and the rise of the welfare state. Section 4 concludes by briefly analyzing the European state development experience in comparative perspective.

2 What Effective Statehood Entails

In this section, I develop a simple conceptual framework to help understand the political conditions required to establish effective statehood.[3] I will use this framework to guide the historical analysis in subsequent sections.

2.1 Conceptualizations

To start, I must conceptualize two elements: state capacity and effective statehood. "State capacity" concerns the state's ability to accomplish its intended policy actions (as described in Section 1). "Effective statehood," in turn, concerns the political arrangements that enable the state to best accomplish its intended policy actions. Thus, effective statehood will enhance state capacity.

---

[3] This framework expands Dincecco (2011, 2015).

My conceptualization of effective statehood draws on a classic statement by James Madison in *The Federalist Papers* (1788). Madison (1788: 257) writes: "In framing a government which is to be administered by men over men, the great difficulty lies in this: you must first enable the government to control the governed; and in the next place oblige it to control itself."

Many current arguments about effective statehood highlight the importance of political conditions akin to those described by Madison, lending credence to his insights. Besley and Persson (2011: 6–7) focus on the state's extractive and productive roles. The former refers to the state's ability to gather revenues from its citizenry – which they label "fiscal capacity," while the latter refers to the state's ability to spend public funds on goods and services which will benefit society – in their parlance, "legal capacity." According to this view, the combination of high fiscal and legal capacity enables the state to take effective action. Acemoglu and Robinson (2012: 79–81) emphasize "inclusive political institutions." They argue that the state must not only be strong enough to provide basic law and order, but must also have a pluralistic political system that broadly distributes power in society and subjects each government branch to limits. North, Wallis, and Weingast (2009: 21–5) define an "open access order" in which the military and police are able to quell violence in society, subject to control by a political system which has internal checks and balances and calls for widespread social support for any political group to stay in charge. Fukuyama (2004: 21–6) distinguishes between "state power" – the government's ability to execute policy and enforce the law, and "state scope" – the different functions that society expects the government to perform (relative to the private sector). In his view, optimal stateness combines high state power with moderate state scope. Acemoglu (2005: 1203–4) describes a "consensually-strong state" whereby society acquiesces to greater taxation in exchange for valued public goods, but only if society is able to readily replace public leaders that underperform their policy mandate – as this political feature promotes state-society consensus to begin with. Hanson (2014: 380–2) draws attention to both the state's ability to project authority on one hand and institutionalized checks on the political executive on the other. Finally, several recent review articles about state development (Dincecco, 2015; Hoffman, 2015a; Bardhan, 2016; Johnson and Koyama, 2017) make use of Madison-style political conditions as analytic building blocks.

Overall, this discussion highlights the enduring influence of the political conditions first described by Madison.

2.2   Political Conditions

To better understand the political conditions required to establish effective statehood, I now break down Madison's classic statement into the two sequential conditions that comprise it: (1) "you must first enable the government to control the governed" and (2) "in the next place oblige it to control itself."

2.2.1   Condition 1: Fiscal Centralization

I start with Condition 1, conceptualizing the state's ability to "control" its citizenry in terms of its power over taxation. I focus on taxation for both theoretical and practical reasons. First, fiscal strength is central to state power. Levi (1988: 2) explains this relationship as follows:

> One major limitation on rule is revenue, the income of the government. The greater the revenue of the state, the more possible it is to extend rule. Revenue enhances the ability of rulers to elaborate the institutions of the state, to bring more people within the domain of those institutions, and to increase the number and variety of the collective goods provided through the state.

A second reason is practical. A main goal of this inquiry is to analyze the historical origins of state capacity. However, there is a general lack of quantitative historical data. Historical fiscal data are in fact available, however, enabling comparisons over time and across states (Drelichman and Voth, 2014: 254).

To satisfy Condition 1 in fiscal terms, the national (central, federal) government must have both the political authority and the administrative ability to implement a standard system of taxation with uniform tax rates throughout its domestic territory.[4] Though basic, this condition strikes at the heart of Levi's (1988: 2) statement above. Without a standard tax system, state revenues will remain small due to the problem of local tax free-riding (which I will describe in Section 3), reducing the state's ability to effectively accomplish its intended policy actions. In this regard, Condition 1 speaks to Besley and Persson's (2013: 51) statement about the importance of taxation to economic development. They write: "The central question in taxation and development is: how does a government go from raising around 10 percent of GDP in taxes to raising around 40 percent?"

What is surprising is how difficult fiscal centralization (and state centralization more generally) can be in practice, no matter how obvious it may appear in theory. In Europe, fiscal centralization took several hundred years. I will describe this process in detail in Section 3. Furthermore, state centralization still hinders many developing nations today. At the extreme is Somalia, which is divided into several hostile clans, none of which can prevail over each other (Acemoglu and Robinson, 2012: 238–43). In the absence of a state with enough resources to secure law and order, life can be very difficult. Fukuyama (2011: 13), for example, writes sardonically: "In Somalia, where a strong central government has not existed since the late 1980s, ordinary individuals may own not just assault rifles but also rocket-propelled grenades, anti-aircraft

---

[4] This condition can accommodate federal systems of government. To illustrate, take the US federal government. Under the Articles of Confederation, Congress was dependent on tax requisitions on individual states (Edling, 2003: 163–74). By contrast, the 1787 Constitution granted Congress the legal authority to uphold a uniform system of taxation throughout the United States (Edling, 2003: 163–74). The US federal government thus meets Condition 1. Fiscal centralization, however, need not imply that the national government has a total monopoly over domestic taxation. For example, individual US states retain legal authority over local tax policy. I discuss decentralized governance in greater detail ahead.

missiles, and tanks. People are free to protect their own families, and indeed are forced to do so."

There is no scholarly consensus about why state centralization is so problematic in the contemporary developing country context. Recently, Acemoglu, Robinson, and Torvik (2016) have provided one explanation. They argue that state centralization improves the ability of citizens to organize and demand public goods. Thus, to preempt effective citizen organization, elites may prefer to maintain fragmented state institutions. In a related manner, Acemoglu, Ticchi, and Vindigni (2011) argue that it may be optimal for elites to create an inefficient state in order to exploit political patronage by bureaucrats and reduce redistributive taxation, while Acemoglu et al. (2016) argue that state-building efforts that place the main emphasis on security objectives may hinder the development of other important governmental institutions (i.e., administrative, fiscal, and legal).

Rethinking Weber

It makes sense to rethink Max Weber's classic definition of the state in light of Condition 1. Weber (1946: 78) writes: "[A] state is a human community that (successfully) claims the monopoly of the legitimate use of physical force within a given territory." To the extent that Weber's definition characterizes an endpoint of the state development process, it is not particularly meaningful for historical-oriented research (Hoffman, 2015a: 306–8). The state's monopoly of violence is the outcome of a hard-fought historical process, rather than a natural starting point for analysis. As Hoffman (2015a: 307) writes:

> Successfully establishing a monopoly of violence is difficult. It requires resources and (at the very least) popular acquiescence, both of which took time for states to get. So, by sticking to Weber's definition, we overlook the centuries of work that states did both to acquire resources and win people over so that the cost of ruling would not be prohibitive.

I will describe this historical process in Section 3.

Decentralized Governance

The standard theory of fiscal federalism argues that – so long as regions are heterogeneous – decentralized governance generates higher social welfare than centralized governance, because local governments are better able to make policy choices that reflect the specific preferences of each jurisdiction (Weingast, 1995: 4–6; Oates, 1999: 1121–2). What this theory takes for granted, however, is that (i) a centralized state exists to begin with and (ii) this state has a Weber-style monopoly of violence (e.g., Huntington, 1968: 7–8). In the context of the post–World War II United States, this theory's underlying assumption of centralized authority makes sense. If we analyze the long stretch of history (or study state centralization in much of the developing world today, as described above), however, then this assumption is no longer viable. O'Brien (2012: 443–4) makes this point as follows:

> Modern liberal political economy maintains that delegation of responsibilities to private enterprise and to local authorities was invariably a cheaper and more efficient strategy to pursue. That view dates, however, from an age when political stability, good order, and geopolitical conflict could be taken as contained at manageable levels. Prior, to say, 1815, little in the historical record suggests that laissez-faire involving limited and more devolved levels of central governance might have increased rates of economic growth.

The main point is that, for (much of) the historical analysis that I will undertake in Section 3, fiscal federalism was not a relevant choice for policy-makers. Rather, the most important historical concern was how to increase state strength and exploit economies of scale (Epstein, 2000: 7–9; Alesina and Spolaore, 2003: 137–40).[5]

---

[5] In a similar manner, policy debate over the state's willingness to tax – versus its ability – was less pertinent historically, because such a debate implicitly assumes that the state has a monopoly of violence. As described above, however, this assumption is not valid for (much of) the historical period under analysis. Likewise, debate over the government's willingness to tax does not seem particularly relevant for developing nations today, many of which cannot

Even today, relatively strong governments face trade-offs between the economic benefits of greater political scale on one hand and the costs of such scale due to local heterogeneity in policy preferences on the other. Treisman (2007: 247–69), for example, finds that the results of the large empirical literature about the economic effects of decentralization are inconclusive. Recently, Boffa, Piolatti, and Ponzetto (2016) have argued that, while decentralization improves local policy choices (given heterogeneous regions), centralization reduces rent extraction by increasing the overall amount of well-informed voters. Furthermore, they argue that several levels of government (e.g., national, state, and county) reduce political accountability, due to less economies of scope. The authors thus conclude that decentralization may not make economic sense.

2.2.2　Condition 2: Institutional Impartiality and Distributive Politics

Madison's classic statement indicates that Condition 1 – fiscal centralization, as I define it – is necessary to establish effective statehood, but is not sufficient. Though fiscal centralization will generate greater revenue (and thereby enhance state power), how can society ensure that the government will spend the new funds in ways that are likely to actually support economic development? To address this question, I now turn to Condition 2 of Madison's statement regarding the government's ability to "control itself."

Institutional Impartiality

For tractability, I break down Condition 2 into two parts. The first part, which I call Sub-condition 2a, concerns the relative impartiality of governance institutions regarding fiscal matters.[6] To satisfy this sub-condition, there must be an institutional player within the

---

even provide basic public goods (as described in Section 1). Rather, this debate seems most pertinent in the context of post-1945 policy differences over taxation and spending across OECD nations (e.g., Alesina, Glaeser, and Sacerdote, 2001; Prescott, 2004). Levi (1988: 4) provides a brief general discussion of the state's incentives to maximize revenue.

[6] I borrow the terminology for Sub-conditions 2a and 2b from Stasavage (2016a).

national government that has the formal political authority to regularly monitor state finances. This sub-condition draws on North and Weingast's (1989: 815–17) view of the historical establishment of parliamentary fiscal supremacy. To provide an effective check on the executive's fiscal actions, parliament must have a permanent governance role – the executive cannot call or disband parliament at will. Furthermore, parliament must have the ability to regularly oversee the state's budget, including authority over taxation, the right to audit previous government spending, and the right to veto new expenditures.

Distributive Politics

While key, Sub-condition 2a – fiscal supremacy by parliament – may not be enough by itself to adequately constrain the executive's fiscal actions. Sub-condition 2b concerns the distributive politics that lay behind parliament's fiscal role. Drawing on Stasavage (2003: 26–50) and Stasavage (2011: 14–16), this sub-condition recognizes that, if parliament is to be an effective monitor of state finances, then such a charge must actually be in the interest of influential parliamentary groups. We may thus think of distributive politics as the sub-condition that gives "teeth" to its institutional impartiality counterpart. Put differently, if the distributive politics sub-condition does not bind, then the potency of parliament's fiscal governance role (Sub-condition 2a) will be reduced. Pincus and Robinson (2014: 205–22), for example, describe the different policy goals of the Whigs and the Tories, the two major political parties in England during the Industrial Revolution. The Whigs favored a relatively strong fiscal state that would promote productivity growth in manufacturing. The Tories, by contrast, favored a smaller fiscal state. According to Pincus and Robinson's argument, if the Whig party had not dominated the English parliament over the eighteenth century, then the government's fiscal strength would not have increased by leaps and bounds.[7]

---

[7] In the spirit of Besley and Persson (2011: 70–2), higher polarization or heterogeneity between different social groups may also make it more difficult for the distributive politics sub-condition to hold, thereby reducing state effectiveness.

Beyond distributive politics, there are other important factors that may influence parliament's ability to constrain the executive's fiscal actions. Cox (2011) highlights the executive's fiscal moral hazard problem. If the executive reaps political benefits when victorious in warfare, for example, but faces few political costs when defeated, then she is more likely to gamble with public funds. To resolve this moral hazard problem, Cox argues that the executive's cabinet ministers must be held politically accountable for the real-world consequences of her policy actions. In turn, cabinet ministers will have the proper incentive to offer prudent advice a priori, thereby improving the quality of the executive's subsequent policy choices. Similarly, Karaman and Pamuk (2013) argue that fiscal supremacy by parliament will only promote state-building for a particular economic structure, namely a commerce-oriented urban economy, while Gelderblom and Jonker (2011) argue that parliamentary reform will only increase fiscal strength if the economy is rich enough to generate new potential tax flows.

Revenue Implications

By improving the state's ability to spend public funds in productive ways, fiscal supremacy by parliament should further facilitate revenue collection (i.e., beyond the effect of fiscal centralization). The logic of this argument runs as follows. Given Condition 2, it is more likely that any new tax funds will be spent on goods and services that will benefit society (versus the executive only). Thus, parliamentary members may be more willing to agree to new tax requests. In this regard, Condition 2 should increase the state's extractive capacity as well as its productive capacity. The well-known saying "no taxation without representation" captures this concept, implying that the state's fiscal strength depends in part on parliamentary governance and fiscal transparency (Besley and Persson, 2013: 56).[8]

---

[8] According to Thomas Paine, parliamentary government was "the most productive machine for taxation ever invented" (as cited by O'Brien, 2011: 427) This type of argument is known as the fiscal contract view of state-building (Bates and Lien, 1985; Levi, 1988: 52–67; North and Weingast, 1989; Hoffman and Rosenthal, 1997; and Timmons, 2005).

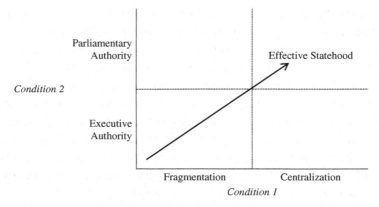

Figure 6 Political Conditions and Effective Statehood

2.2.3   Effective Statehood

In this subsection, I have broken down Madison's classic statement to identify the political conditions required to achieve effective statehood. Condition 1 indicates that there must be fiscal centralization. Condition 2 is divided into two parts. Sub-condition 2a indicates that parliament must have the fiscal authority to regularly check the executive's actions (institutional impartiality), while Sub-condition 2b indicates that influential groups in parliament must have the incentive to actually exercise this authority (distributive politics). Taken together, Conditions 1 and 2 imply that the state will be able to (i) gather enough revenue to accomplish its intended policy actions and (ii) spend public funds in ways that are more likely to support market-oriented economic development (versus wasteful spending).[9] In this manner, the state will be effective (Figure 6). I will use this simple framework to guide the historical analysis in Section 3.

---

[9] In a similar way, Aghion et al. (2016) argue that the relationship between taxation and economic performance is a function of political corruption. If such corruption is low, then taxation can bring economic benefits through the efficient provision of market infrastructure.

2.3 Alternative Political Structures

Effective statehood may promote market-oriented economic development through several channels (as described in Subsection 1.2). To conclude this section, I briefly evaluate the economic potential of two alternative political structures: autocracy and stateless society.

2.3.1 Autocracy

With respect to the conceptual framework described above, we may define autocracy in terms of a political regime in which Condition 1 holds, but Condition 2 does not. According to this definition, an autocrat will have both the political authority and administrative ability to gather enough revenue and accomplish her intended policy actions, but will not face any effective parliamentary checks. To cast this political regime type in terms of Madison's classic statement, autocracy is powerful enough to "control the governed," but has no institutional obligation to "control itself."

Given that Condition 2 should improve the state's ability to spend public funds on goods and services that will promote market-oriented economic development (versus wasteful spending on the executive only), we may think that economic performance under autocracy should be worse than under an effective state. Acemoglu and Robinson (2012: 83–4) provide the example of Joseph Mobutu, the autocratic ruler of the Democratic Republic of the Congo between 1965 and 1997, who spent great amounts of public money on himself, including for a palace in his rural hometown of Gbadolite, replete with a runway big enough for a supersonic jet. Meanwhile, the Congo's economy declined.

At the very least, the conceptual framework suggests that economic performance under autocracy should be less predictable than under an effective state, depending on the executive's (idiosyncratic) tolerance for wasteful spending. The evidence supports this conclusion. North, Wallis, and Weingast (2009: 3–6) analyze economic growth rates over 1950–2004 for 180-plus nations. They argue that autocratic regimes ("the natural state," in their parlance) are poorer than effective states ("open access orders") because autocratic regimes are more vulnerable to negative economic shocks. Similarly, Besley and Kudamatsu (2008: 453) find that economic performance today is more likely to be very good or very bad under autocracy than under democracy.

How to account for China? Over the past several decades, China has experienced rapid economic development (Zhu, 2012: 103). It now has the world's second-largest economy (Zhu, 2012: 103). Yet China was autocratic throughout this development period (Besley and Kudamatsu, 2008: 487). Acemoglu and Robinson (2012: 93–4) provide one explanation for this phenomenon. They argue that an autocracy such as China can achieve economic growth – at least for a time – by exploiting the state's power to move surplus labor in agriculture into (more productive) industry. According to this view, economic growth under autocracy will inevitably reach a limit, once unemployment in agriculture ends. The economic decline of the Soviet Union in the 1970s illustrates this phenomenon (Allen, 2003: 211). If Acemoglu and Robinson's argument is correct, then the relevant question with respect to China becomes: when will the logic of economic growth under autocracy attain its intrinsic limit? Put differently, will any such limit be reached over say the next 10 years, or is this limit decades or more away?

Besley and Kudamatsu (2008: 455–67) provide an alternative explanation for economic development under autocracy: government accountability. They argue that a nation's economic performance depends on whether the state's policy actions support goods and services that will actually benefit society. To promote effective policy, the government in charge must be held accountable. In terms of the conceptual framework described above, Condition 2 – namely, effective parliamentary checks on executive behavior – helps secure such accountability. In autocracy, however, such checks are not present. Here Besley and Kudamatsu argue that government accountability is contingent on the ability of government insiders – the "selectorate" (Bueno de Mesquita et al., 2003: 41–3) – to remove poor-performing executives. If the selectorate's power does not depend on whether the current executive stays in office, then government accountability can occur even in the absence of effective parliamentary checks, thereby improving economic performance. Unlike Acemoglu and Robinson's conclusion as described above, economic growth under autocracy need not reach any inevitable limit, so long as the selectorate's power remains independent of the executive in charge. The selectorate in China is the Politburo, the group of 25 individuals that oversees the Communist Party. According to Besley and Kudamatsu (2008: 487–8), the Politburo has been effective at promoting competent leaders and replacing poor ones since the mid-1970s.[10]

Overall, this brief discussion suggests that economic development may in fact occur under autocracy, but that economic performance (i) should at the very least be more unpredictable and (ii) may be worse on average than under an effective state, due to the reliance on somewhat ad hoc constraints (versus effective parliamentary checks) on the executive's ability to productively spend public funds.

2.3.2   Stateless Society

Given a long enough time horizon, repeated interactions among relatively far-sighted individuals can facilitate self-enforced cooperative behavior even in the absence of the state. This result is commonly known as the folk theorem. Greif (1993) shows how

---

[10] Besley and Kudamatsu's argument suggests that, for specific cases such as post-1976 China, state capacity may be relatively high even if Condition 2 is not satisfied. Put differently, effective statehood may not always be necessary to increase state capacity, so long as an autocratic government can identify an enduring institutional solution to hold itself accountable. This insight may help make sense of Cheibub's (1998) result that tax/GDP ratios did not significantly differ between autocratic and democratic regimes worldwide over 1970–1990. However, it is not obvious how widespread "accountable" autocratic regimes actually are. Besley and Kudamatsu (2008: 468–77), for example, identify just 12 core "successful" autocratic regimes out of more than 300 total political regimes worldwide since 1800 (or less than 4 percent of all regimes). High state capacity under "accountable" autocratic regimes does not therefore appear to be a particularly common real-world outcome.

such social cooperation promoted medieval Mediterranean trade by Maghribi traders in the presence of weak state legal institutions.

Self-enforced cooperation, however, has important economic limitations. Bates (2010: 29–32) argues that cooperative behavior in a stateless society depends on retaliation threats. Family members are honor-bound to seek revenge for property rights violations, curtailing theft. This logic of revenge, however, promotes a hair-trigger society. Furthermore, revenge-oriented violence has the tendency to endure once triggered. Thus, to safeguard peaceful social relations, individuals will prefer to all live in relative poverty, reducing the incentive for theft.

Similarly, Boix (2015: 54–5) argues that social equality is necessary to sustain cooperative behavior. If one group has a significant military advantage, for example, then it will try to dominate the others. In this context, technological innovations can only occur if they will equally benefit all social groups. Given that many inventions do not lend themselves to replication or sharing, innovation will falter, reducing development prospects.

Pinker (2011: 52–3) shows evidence that non-state society was in fact more violent than state-oriented society. Across 25-plus non-states (hunter-gathers, hunter-horticulturalists), the average yearly death rate was 524 per 100,000 individuals. By contrast, this rate was only 60 per 100,000 individuals for all deaths worldwide from wars, genocides, purges, and (man-made) famines over the twentieth century. Scholars argue that large-scale civil violence brings high economic and social costs (Blattman and Miguel, 2010: 4; Collier et al., 2013: 13–38).

Overall, this brief discussion suggests that the economic performance of a stateless society will be stagnant at best.

3   Historical Origins of State Capacity

The simple conceptual framework in Section 2 characterizes the basic political conditions required for effective statehood. This section analyzes long-run state development in Western Europe in light of this conceptual framework, with a focus on three main inflection points: the rise of the city-state, the rise of the nation-state, and the rise of the welfare state.

3.1 Rise of the City-State

3.1.1 Political Fragmentation and Warfare

The starting point for my analysis is the aftermath of the fall of the Carolingian Empire over the 800s. The demise of this empire resulted in a high level of political fragmentation (Strayer, 1970: 15). Such fragmentation was long-lasting. For example, there were upwards of 500 independent states in late medieval Europe (Tilly, 1992: 45). Furthermore, average medieval state size was small, at roughly 25,000 square kilometers (Tilly, 1992: 45).

High political fragmentation made instability and warfare more likely (van Zanden, 2009: 34). In fact, warfare was a main feature of Europe's historical landscape (Tilly, 1992: 72, 74; Parker, 1996: 1; Hoffman, 2015b: 21–2). Dincecco and Onorato (2017: chapter 2) identify more than 850 major military conflicts fought on land in Europe over 1000–1799, for an average of 100-plus conflicts per century. Figure 7 displays the locations of all such conflicts, the locus of which took place in the central corridor that runs from Belgium and the Netherlands to Northern Italy through parts of France and Germany. Beyond high political fragmentation, the quest for glory by rulers (Hoffman, 2015b: 19, 24–6) and scarce territory (Hale, 1985: 22–3) also help explain why historical warfare was endemic in Europe.

Endemic warfare is a prominent explanation for institutional change in European history (Bates and Lien, 1985: 54–7; Mann, 1986: 125–32; Downing, 1992: 18–55; Tilly, 1992: 67–95; Ertman, 1997: 74–87; Stasavage, 2016b: 154–6). Tilly's (1975: 42) famous expression is: "War made the state, and the state made war." The basic logic of this argument runs as follows. Historical warfare was very expensive (e.g., Hoffman, 2015b: 19, 21–2). To secure new revenue, sovereign rulers in medieval Europe were willing to grant various local privileges – including urban self-governance and property rights protections (Blockmans and t'Hart, 2013: 426) – as

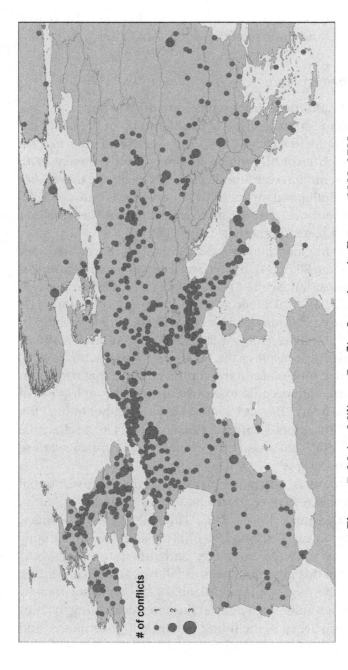

Figure 7 Major Military Conflict Locations in Europe, 1000–1799

Notes: 856 land-based conflicts. Dot sizes indicate the number of conflicts geocoded to each specific location.

Source: Dincecco and Onorato (2017).

well as establish national-level representative political institutions, both of which gave elite taxpayers formal roles in governance matters. By relinquishing (partial) political control, rulers could raise new funds and enhance military might.[11] Stasavage (2016b: 155) finds a significant relationship between war frequency and parliamentary activity for a panel of 20-plus European states over 1250–1800.

3.1.2 City-States versus Territorial States

According to the conceptual framework in Section 2, effective statehood calls for fiscal centralization (Condition 1) along with institutional impartiality (Sub-condition 2a) and distributive politics (Sub-condition 2b). We may divide states in medieval Europe into two basic types: compact city-states and larger territorial states (which we may think of as precursors to subsequent nation-states). A key governance problem in this historical context was geographical scale (Stasavage, 2011: 14–16). Medieval territorial states could not satisfy Condition 1 due to local institutional fragmentation within them (Epstein, 2000: 13–16; Dincecco, 2011: 10–13). I will discuss this problem in greater detail in the next subsection. Similarly, medieval territorial states could not satisfy Condition 2a due to high historical communications and travel costs. Geographical scale made it very difficult for representatives in medieval territorial states to attend parliamentary meetings (which may have taken place in distant capitals), and for constituents to monitor the performance of their representatives (Blockmans, 1998: 37; Stasavage, 2011: 14–16).

To identify the medieval origins of effective statehood in Western Europe, therefore, we must look to city-states, and not to territorial states. Due to their compact size, city-states were more likely to have both the political authority and the administrative ability to implement a standard system of internal taxation (Condition 1). Similarly,

---

[11] Gennaioli and Voth (2015) argue that warfare only promoted state development (including parliamentary government) when military success became dependent on high revenue, a sea change which they claim did not occur until after the post-1500 military revolution (Parker, 1996: 1–2).

given trivial communications and travel costs, parliamentary representatives were more likely to meet frequently in city-states (Condition 2a). Finally, Stasavage (2011: 14–16) argues that it was more likely for influential groups in parliament to actually exercise their formal authority over fiscal matters in city-states (Condition 2b). In medieval Europe, merchants tended to politically dominate city-states, while the landowning aristocracy generally dominated territorial states. Given their commercial and financial interests, urban merchants were more likely than landowning aristocrats to have liquid forms of wealth, which they could invest in public debt. In order to protect such investments, moreover, urban merchants had a strong incentive to monitor public finances through parliamentary oversight (which, given frequent meetings, they could do effectively). By contrast, landowning aristocrats outnumbered individuals with large amounts of liquid wealth in territorial states, making it less likely that such individuals could readily influence parliamentary fiscal decisions.

3.1.3 Fiscal Implications

The fiscal evidence supports the argument that the distant roots of effective statehood in Western Europe are to be found in city-states rather than territorial states. The most systematic fiscal data available are from Stasavage (2011: 29–43), who constructs a panel database of nominal interest rates on long-term public debt for 19 city-states and 12 territorial states over 1250–1750.[12] Given endemic warfare, the ability to borrow enabled medieval states to respond quickly to military imperatives that were important to their survival (Stasavage, 2011: 25–9).

Figure 8 provides a snapshot of the historical evolution of public debt in Western Europe. Two key patterns distinguish city-states from territorial states. First, city-states established long-term public debt well before territorial states. Arras was the first sample

---

[12] To the best of my knowledge, systematic revenue data are not available for the medieval era. However, such data are available for the early modern era (Dincecco, 2011; Karaman and Pamuk, 2013), which I will analyze in the next subsection.

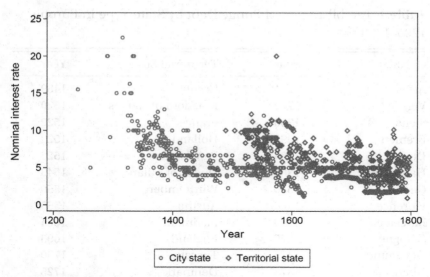

Figure 8 Evolution of State Type and Public Debt in Europe,
1200–1800
Notes: Nominal interest rate is for long-term public debt. Data
are for 19 historical city states and 12 historical territorial states.
Table 1 lists the included states. Total yearly observations: 1,198.
Source: Stasavage (2011).

city-state to take out a long-term loan in 1241 (Table 1). By 1400,
nearly 80 percent of sample city-states had created long-term
public debt. In contrast, the first sample territorial state to issue
long-term public debt was Castile in 1489 – nearly 250 years after
the city-state of Arras. Second, city-states could borrow on more
favorable terms than territorial states. During the era in which both
state types had established long-term public debt, nominal interest
rates were lower on average for city-states than territorial states.

The statistical analysis in Stasavage (2011: 77–93) provides
econometric proof that city-states had significantly better access
to credit than territorial states. He controls for time-varying observables including returns on land rents, urbanization, and common
structural changes after 1500.

Table 1 Establishment of Public Debt by State Type in Europe, 1200–1800

City State	Year	Territorial State	Year
Arras	1241	Castile	1489
Venice	1262	Kingdom of Naples	1520
Siena	1290	France	1522
Bremen	1295	Holland	1522
Douai	1295	Papal States	1526
Hamburg	1308	Duchy of Milan	1543
Genoa	1340	Württemberg	1550
Florence	1347	Austria	1555
Barcelona	1360	Piedmont	1684
Cologne	1375	England	1693
Dortmund	1375	Tuscany	1700
Ghent	1375	Denmark	1725
Nuremberg	1381		
Basel	1383		
Zurich	1386		
Mainz	1415		
Bruges	1489		
Geneva	1538		
Bologna	1555		

Notes: The year column refers to the first year for which data exists for the nominal interest rate on long-term public debt.
Source: Stasavage (2011).

3.1.4 Economic Implications

By reducing the likelihood of expropriation by predatory rulers, effective governance by medieval city-states could promote economic development (Blockmans and t'Hart, 2013: 426). According to Max Weber (1958: 181–90), secure property rights were a defining feature of the medieval city. In turn, the urban legal environment may have been more conducive to private investment in new machinery, greater education, and/or technological innovations (as described in Subsection 1.2). van Zanden, Buringh, and

Bosker (2012) find a positive correlation between regional parliamentary activity – which they argue placed institutional checks on royal power – and economic development for 30-plus regional parliaments in Europe over 800–1800.[13] Similarly, human capital levels were higher in the medieval city than in the countryside (Mokyr, 1995: 10–11; van Zanden, 2009: 86). Finally, many important historical inventions took place in urban centers, including in cartography, chemicals, clock-making, gun-making, hydraulics, instrument-making, medicine, metalwork, optical utensils, paper-making, printing, textiles, and shipping (Bairoch, 1988: 336; Mokyr, 1995: 8–9).

Stasavage (2014) argues that medieval urban property rights were a double-edged sword, because urban capital owners were eventually able to implement entry limits into their professions, blocking further technological innovations. Drawing on a sample of 170-plus urban centers in Europe over 1000–1800, he shows evidence that city autonomy – a proxy for local property rights – promoted economic growth over the first century of self-governance, but reduced it over the long run. Here we must take care to discern between the growth effects of property rights institutions for any individual city-state and the overall growth effect of technological competition between urban centers. Mokyr (1995: 17–19), for example, argues that, even if individual city-states were eventually subject to entry limits by the local oligarchy, the cumulative impact of technological innovations across urban centers as a whole was of major importance for long-run economic development in Europe.

3.1.5 Geographical Endowments

To conclude this subsection, it makes sense to analyze the extent to which the causal logic may have run the other way, from prior economic development to local political representation. According to this type of argument (e.g., Rokkan, 1975: 575–91; Tilly, 1992:

---

[13] Other statistical works that document the relationship between political institutions that checked royal power and long-run economic development in Europe include De Long and Shleifer (1993), Acemoglu, Johnson, and Robinson (2005), and Cox (2017).

17–19), the central corridor that runs from Belgium and the Netherlands to Northern Italy through eastern France and western Germany had favorable geographical endowments, including high-quality soil and easy access to river trade routes. High-quality soil improved agricultural productivity, generating the food surplus that first made urban agglomerations possible. Facilitated by river trade routes, urban agglomerations in turn promoted commercial activity. Over time, economic agglomeration effects enabled urban leaders to build upon their early economic success. According to this view, representative government – and thus property rights protection – in medieval city-states was a result (rather than a cause) of prior economic growth.[14]

While the geographical endowments argument is plausible, it cannot fully account for the development of effective governance by medieval city-states for at least four reasons.

First, the geographical endowments argument overlooks the Roman legacy of medieval city locations (Verhulst, 1999: 1, 21–3; Boone, 2013: 221–2). Roman towns were often founded to achieve bureaucratic and military objectives specific to the ancient context (Verhulst, 1999: 23). By serving as enduring meeting points, however, Roman fortifications were "footprints of history" (Bleakley and Lin, 2015: 558) which influenced the placement of medieval towns above and beyond local geographical endowments.

Second, the geographical endowments argument overlooks the accidental partitioning of the Carolingian Empire (Ganshof, 1971: 289–98; Stasavage, 2011: 95–100). The apparent basis for this partitioning was the need for an equal territorial split between Charlemagne's three heirs, and not contemporaneous ethnic, linguistic, political, or religious borders (Ganshof, 1971: 289–98). The former border zones of West and East Francia became large and stable kingdoms, while the former Carolingian core of

---

[14] Recently, Abramson and Boix (2015) have provided statistical evidence in support of this argument, though Cox (2017: appendix C) offers what appears to be a plausible critique of their fixed effects regression analysis.

Lotharingia – the central corridor as described above – became politically fragmented, making instability and warfare more likely. In this context, political bargains which granted local privileges (i.e., urban self-governance, property rights protections) in exchange for new military funds may have been particularly attractive, regardless of geographical endowments.

Third, the geographical endowments argument overlooks the potential for endogenous food production. Over the medium run, medieval urban centers could make technological innovations such as convertible husbandry that improved agricultural productivity (Bairoch, 1988: 336–40; Mokyr, 1995: 11). Furthermore, urban centers could exploit commercial agriculture and external trade to increase food production (Smith, 2007: 313; Rosenthal and Wong, 2011: 46). In such ways, urban centers could overcome indigenous geographical shortcomings (de Vries, 1984: 244).

Finally, the geographical endowments argument overlooks the cross-regional evidence. The level of economic development in Western Europe in the year 1000 was significantly lower than in China and somewhat lower than in the Middle East (Stasavage, 2016b: 153–4). If economic growth promoted representative government, therefore, then we would expect China to have been a historical parliamentary leader. However, representative government only developed in Western Europe.

Overall, this evidence indicates that geographical endowments and prior economic growth cannot fully explain the emergence of effective governance by medieval city-states.

3.2 Rise of the Nation-State

I have argued in the previous subsection that the historical bedrock of effective statehood in Western Europe is to be found in medieval city-states, which were more likely than their territorial counterparts to satisfy Conditions 1 and 2 of the conceptual framework. I now turn to the second key inflection point in long-run state development in Western Europe: the rise of nation-states (which in several cases were outgrowths of their territorial state predecessors).

3.2.1   Local Tax Free-Riding

By the start of the 1500s, many nation-states in Europe had domestic territorial borders that were relatively similar to their modern-day borders (Dincecco, 2011: 10–12). For example, modern-day France has inherited the territorial borders first established by Louis XI (reign, 1461–83) (Dincecco, 2011: 10). However, early modern nation-states did not satisfy any of the conditions – fiscal centralization, institutional impartiality, and distributive politics – for effective statehood.

Contrary to the conventional wisdom, sovereign rulers in early modern Europe were generally weak (Strayer, 1970: 51–3; Brewer, 1989: 6–7; Epstein, 2000: 13). Epstein (2000: 14) writes: "The strength of a monarch's theoretical claims to absolutist rule was frequently inversely proportional to his de facto powers." Due to endemic political fragmentation and warfare, sovereign rulers often relinquished (partial) political control to local elites in exchange for greater funds for the military (as described in the previous subsection). Such political bargains, however, enabled city-states to obstruct subsequent centralization efforts at the national level (Blockmans, 1989; 752–3; Epstein, 2000: 8–9). Generally speaking, we may view early modern nation-states as "mosaics" built upon a medley of local institutional structures (Strayer, 1970: 53; Epstein, 2000: 14–15). Brewer (1989: 6), for example, describes the political institutions of early modern France as follows:

> As the state expanded it was confronted by a highly developed and intractable regionalism institutionalized in the form of local law and regional assemblies and sustained by powerful local notables. It could only superimpose its control on a number of entrenched and thriving institutions . . . .. This compromise between regional and state power produced a many-layered administration linking disparate provincial practices to a national system of government. Particularism was built into the French state apparatus.

In early modern Europe, there was a revolution in military tactics, strategy, army size, technology, and impact (Parker,

1996: 1–2; Gennaioli and Voth, 2015: 1413–14), making military success far more dependent on high revenue (Blockmans, 1989; 751–2; Gennaioli and Voth, 2015).[15] Local institutional fragmentation, however, made it difficult for national governments to extract greater funds. Put differently, sovereign rulers faced a stubborn tax free-riding problem (Dincecco, 2009: 51–2, 2011: 12).[16] Local elites were likely to oppose national-level fiscal reforms that would undermine their traditional tax rights, because control over taxation was a fundamental part of self-governance. Given state weakness, sovereign rulers could not simply impose a standard system of taxation throughout their domestic territory (as Condition 1 calls for), but were compelled to bargain region by region over local tax rates. In this historical context, local elites hoped to free-ride on outside tax contributions, paying less while other regions took up the slack. Since elites across all regions free-rode in this way, national governments could only extract low revenue per capita.

To further elucidate this historical tax free-riding problem, we can cast it in terms of a simple prisoner's dilemma (Table 2). For exposition, say that there are just two players: regional elite 1 and regional elite 2. Each elite group can oppose or endorse national-level fiscal reform. From the perspective of society as a whole, the best outcome occurs when both elite groups endorse fiscal reform. This outcome – (Endorse, Endorse) – is Pareto optimal, because there is no other outcome that is strictly favored by one elite group that is at least as favorable to the other group (Ostrom, 1990: 3–5). The intuition is that, after undertaking fiscal reform, the national government can gather enough resources to provide the sorts of

---

[15] Early modern governments spent 40–80 percent of annual funds on the military, not counting funds spent on subsidizing allies and on servicing debts for past wars (Hoffman, 2015b: 21–2). In seventeenth-century France, for example, median annual military expenditures were 80 percent of the government's budget (Hoffman, 2015b: 23).

[16] In early modern Europe, this type of fiscal free-riding problem went part and parcel with the free-riding problem related to market exchange as described in Subsection 1.2 (Epstein, 2000: 9; Dincecco, 2011: 14).

Table 2 Tax Free-Riding in Old Regime Europe

		Regional Elite 2	
		Oppose	Endorse
Regional Elite 1	Endorse	*l, h*	*c, c*
	Oppose	*d, d*	*h, l*

Notes: The action "Oppose" refers to opposition to national-level fiscal reform, while the action "Endorse" refers to endorsement of it. Payoffs are ordered: (Regional Elite 1, Regional Elite 2). Payoff values are $h > c > d > l$.

basic public goods (i.e., rules of the game, competitive and free domestic market) that promote widespread economic development. The paradox, however, is that each elite group has a dominant incentive to free-ride on the other group (Ostrom, 1990: 3–5). Namely, each elite group will oppose fiscal reform in the hope that the other will take up the slack. Both elite groups will attempt to free-ride, and the outcome that actually occurs – (Oppose, Oppose) – leaves the two elite groups worse off than if both had endorsed.[17]

To overcome this free-riding problem, nation-states in Europe sought both the political authority and the administrative ability to implement a standard system of taxation throughout their domestic territory, rather than bargain region by region. If successful, then per capita revenue extracted by national governments would increase (so long as local tax rates were equalized at high enough levels). Fiscal centralization, however, was a long and difficult process. To illustrate, take early modern France. White (2001: 66) writes: "Several times an invigorated Crown initiated new reforms to centralize and simplify the tax system, but in the long run the government had limited success in altering the basic tax structure."

---

[17] Repeated interactions may facilitate cooperative outcomes in the prisoner's dilemma (i.e., the folk theorem). However, we may think that high historical communications and travel costs (Stasavage, 2011: 14–16) reduced the scope for such grassroots cooperation.

French tax rates were uneven across space. For example, elites in the center and north of early modern France were exempt from the *taille*, an important direct tax on land, while elites in the south were only responsible for the *taille* for particular land holdings (Dincecco, 2011: 10–11). In the 1660s, Finance Minister Jean-Baptiste Colbert undertook well-known fiscal reforms (Johnson, 2006: 979–81). His "success" was to divide France into (only) eight domestic tariff zones (Dincecco, 2011: 11). Yet local tariffs did not disappear. Within the largest domestic customs zone – the *Cinq Grosses Fermes* – there were still five local tariffs (Dincecco, 2011: 11). Fiscal centralization would not take place in France until more than 100 years later.

Dating Fiscal Centralization

Swift and permanent structural changes to national-level fiscal institutions typically took place in Western Europe from the French Revolution onward (1789–99) (Dincecco, 2011: 22).[18] Conquests by the French military were important catalysts for such radical structural changes (Woolf, 1991: 96–115; Acemoglu et al., 2011: 3289–90; O'Brien, 2011: 436). England was an important exception to this timing (Brewer, 1989: 3–7; Epstein, 2000: 14; O'Brien, 2011). There the Norman Conquest of 1066 undercut local political authority and established a high level of institutional centralization (Brewer, 1989: 3–4).[19] Table 3 dates fiscal centralization for 11 historical sovereign governments in Western Europe.

---

[18] Fiscal changes did in fact occur in early modern Europe (Johnson, 2006; Karaman and Pamuk, 2013: 623; Johnson and Koyama, 2014). However, the magnitudes of pre-1789 fiscal gains by nation-states were relatively small (Dincecco, 2015: 905).

[19] For simplicity, I generally use the term "England" rather than "Britain" or the "United Kingdom," though England conjoined with Wales in 1536, Scotland in 1707, and Ireland in 1800 (Dincecco, 2011: 14). Historical levels of institutional centralization were higher for England than for Britain as a whole (Brewer, 1988: 5–6).

Table 3 Fiscal Centralization in European History

	Year	Event
England	1066	Establishment of uniform rule after Norman Conquest
France	1790	Major administrative reforms during French Revolution
Belgium	1795	Major administrative reforms after French annexation
Piedmont	1802	Major administrative reforms after French annexation
Netherlands	1806	Major administrative reforms under French control
Prussia	1806	Major administrative reforms after French defeat in battle
Spain	1845	Major administrative reforms after Moderate Coup of 1843
Austria	1848	Major administrative reforms during Year of Revolutions
Portugal	1859	Major administrative reforms after Revolutionary Era
Sweden	1861	Abolition of traditional tax system
Denmark	1903	Abolition of traditional tax system

Notes: Fiscal centralization is the year in which the national government first established both the political authority and the administrative ability to implement a standard system of taxation with uniform tax rates throughout its domestic territory. See text for further details.
Sources: Dincecco (2011) and Dincecco, Federico, and Vindigni (2011) for Piedmont.

3.2.2 Executive Checks

Fiscal centralization often took place in the context of wide-reaching institutional reforms that abolished the traditional fiscal, legal, and political powers of local elites. Still, by 1815, most nation-states in Western Europe could not yet satisfy Condition 2 regarding institutional impartiality (Sub-condition 2a) and distributive politics (Sub-condition 2b). National-level representative political institutions did exist, but they did not generally place effective checks on executive power. As described in the previous subsection, the problem of geographic scale made it very difficult for representatives to attend parliamentary meetings, which may have taken place in far-flung capitals. Furthermore, national parliaments were only called at the ruler's request and did not always meet regularly (Stasavage, 2011: 47–69). Finally, sovereign fiscal authority was typically divided between parliament and the ruler (Hoffman and Rosenthal, 1997: 32–8). While parliamentary elites exerted control over taxation, rulers exerted control over spending. Given this institutional context, parliamentary elites were very hesitant to fulfill new tax requests by rulers, because they feared that new funds would be spent in wasteful ways such as military adventures (Dincecco, 2011: 26–7). The problem of royal moral hazard in warfare (Cox, 2011) – whereby rulers saw clear upsides from victory, but few downsides from defeat – exacerbated the fundamental dilemma of divided fiscal authority between parliamentary elites and rulers. To avoid parliament, rulers turned to fiscal predation, including forced loans, the sales of government lands and offices, and the confiscation of private property (e.g., North and Weingast, 1989: 808–12).

Dating Institutional Impartiality

Institutional impartiality (Sub-condition 2a) typically took place decades after fiscal centralization over the 1800s (Figure 9). From the aftermath of the Treaty of Paris (1815) to the mid-nineteenth century, there were six cases of institutional impartiality among sample nation-states. Similarly, there were five such cases between 1850 and the eve of World War I. There were, however, two important exceptions to this timing: England and the Dutch Republic. The Glorious Revolution of 1688 in England is the archetypical example of the establishment of fiscal supremacy by parliament (North and Weingast, 1989). Similarly, the Dutch Republic (1572–1795) is often deemed a constitutional regime (e.g., De Long and Shleifer, 1993: 683). Table 4 dates the establishment of

Table 4 Institutional Impartiality in European History

	Year	Event
Netherlands	1572	Establishment of Dutch Republic (1572–1795) after revolt from Spain
	1848	Implementation of new constitution during Year of Revolutions
France	1830–48	Establishment of constitutional monarchy after Revolution of 1830
	1870	Formation of constitutional regime during war with Prussia
England	1688	Establishment of constitutional monarchy during Glorious Revolution
Belgium	1831	Founded as constitutional monarchy after Revolution of 1830
Denmark	1848	Establishment of constitutional monarchy during Year of Revolutions
Piedmont	1848	Establishment of constitutional monarchy during Year of Revolutions
Prussia	1848	Establishment of constitutional monarchy during Year of Revolutions
Portugal	1851	Establishment of constitutional monarchy after Revolutionary Era
Sweden	1866	Introduction of bicameral legislature
Austria	1867	Establishment of constitutional monarchy after defeat by Prussia
Spain	1876	Establishment of constitutional monarchy after civil war

Notes: Institutional impartiality is the year in which the national parliament first gained the political authority to regularly monitor state finances. See text for further details.
Sources: Dincecco (2011) and Dincecco, Federico, and Vindigni (2011) for Piedmont.

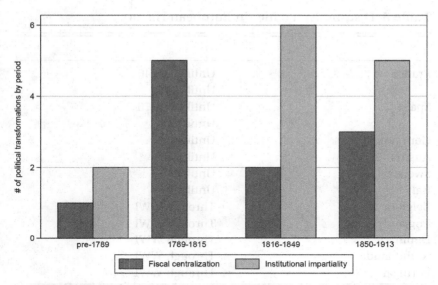

Figure 9 Political Transformations by Period, 1650–1913
Notes: Fiscal centralization is the year in which the national government first established both the political authority and the administrative ability to implement a standard system of taxation with uniform tax rates throughout its domestic territory.
Institutional impartiality is the year in which the national parliament first gained the political authority to regularly monitor state finances. See text and Tables 3 and 4 for further details.
Sources: Dincecco (2011) and Dincecco, Federico, and Vindigni (2011) for Piedmont.

institutional impartiality across sample sovereign governments in Western Europe.[20]

[20] An alternative way to code Sub-condition 2a would be to replace "institutional impartiality" (as defined in Subsection 2.2) with "parliamentary responsibility" according to Przeworski, Asadurian, and Bohlken (2012), which they define to be a political regime in which (i) the actions for which government ministers are responsible are not specified ex ante, (ii) the procedures according to which ministers can be held accountable take the form of a no-confidence vote, (iii) the only sanction to which ministers may be subject is to leave office, and (iv) ministerial responsibility is collective (versus individual). Note that the use of

Table 5 Distributive Politics in European History

	Years
France	Until 1831–46
	Until 1870
Spain	Until 1869–76
	Until 1890
Germany	Until 1871
Austria	Until 1907
Sweden	Until 1909
Italy	Until 1913
Belgium	Through WWI
England	Through WWI
Denmark	Through WWI
Netherlands	Through WWI
Portugal	Through WWI

Notes: Distributive politics refers to a parliamentary regime in which there is restricted and unequal male suffrage as defined by (i) tax payment minima and/or literacy requirements, and/or (ii) the holding of indirect elections, and/or (iii) the lack of secret ballots. This definition follows Stasavage (2016a: 11–12). The year column refers to the year through which distributive politics (according to the definition above) were kept intact.
Sources: Flora (1983) and Caramani (2000) for Portugal and Spain.

Dating Distributive Politics

To operationalize the dating of distributive politics (Sub-condition 2b), I follow Stasavage (2016a: 11–12). In the spirit of his definition, distributive politics refers to a parliamentary regime in which there is restricted and unequal male suffrage as defined by (i) tax payment minima and/or literacy requirements, and/or (ii) the holding of indirect elections, and/or (iii) the lack of secret ballots. Table 5 dates the years through which distributive politics as defined above

this alternative, however, only strengthens the descriptive results in Figures 11 and 16.

were kept intact among sample sovereign governments in Western Europe. Distributive politics, according to this definition, typically held through the start of the twentieth century, with three exceptions: France (1830–46 and 1870 onward), Germany (1871 onward), and Spain (1869–76 and 1890 onward).

3.2.3 Fiscal Implications

Figure 10 provides a snapshot of the historical evolution of sovereign revenue in early modern Europe. To construct this figure, I draw on panel data from Dincecco (2011) and Dincecco, Federico, and Vindigni (2011). Two main patterns stand out. First, consistent with the discussion above, the establishment of effective states at the national level did not become widespread until the mid-nineteenth century. Old Regime nation-states rarely satisfied any of the conditions (i.e., fiscal centralization, institutional impartiality, distributive politics) for effective statehood. As described above, the exception was England, which established an effective state by the end of the seventeenth century. The sole pre-1800 time series in grey squares in Figure 10 corresponds with this polity. Second, per capita revenue was much higher once Conditions 1 and 2 were satisfied (including for pre-1800 England). Average revenue under centralized regimes (Condition 1) was 6.54 gold grams per capita, more the double than the Old Regime average of 2.43 gold grams (Figure 11).[21] Similarly, average revenue under effective states (Conditions 1 and 2) was 12.15 gold grams per capita, nearly double the average for regimes that were centralized only, and five times the average under the Old Regime.

The statistical analyses in Dincecco (2011: 82–107) and Dincecco and Katz (2016: 206–9) provide econometric evidence that more effective national-level states were able to extract significantly greater revenue than their Old Regime counterparts. For example,

---

[21] To facilitate cross-polity comparisons, all currency units are in gold grams (Dincecco, 2011: 48). This conversion should reduce inflation effects, given that the global gold stock was relatively stable through the mid-nineteenth century (Dincecco, 2011: 48).

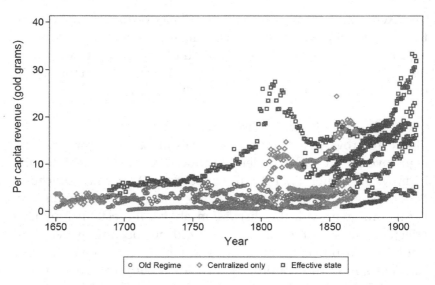

Figure 10 Evolution of Regime Type and Revenue in Europe,
1650–1913
Notes: Data are for 11 historical sovereign governments: Austria,
Belgium, Denmark, France, England, Dutch Republic/
Netherlands, Piedmont, Portugal, Prussia, Spain, and Sweden.
Total yearly observations: 1,502.
Sources: Dincecco (2011) and Dincecco, Federico, and Vindigni
(2011) for Piedmont.

Dincecco (2011: 82–107) controls for polity fixed effects along with
a broad range of time-varying observables, including military alli-
ances, external conflicts, civil conflicts, urbanization rates, sovereign defaults, the gold standard, the global gold stock, and Old
Regime institutional structures.

Greater revenue extraction by sovereign governments was not
simply a by-product of economic growth.[22] Figure 12 plots per

---

[22] Similarly, revenues from overseas colonies cannot wholly explain historical fiscal
development in Western Europe (O'Brien, 2011: 415). O'Brien (2011: 415) sum-
marizes this evidence as follows: "Total flows of colonial tribute into the coffers
of governments of the Ottoman, Mughal, Qing, Romanov, Austrian-Habsburg,

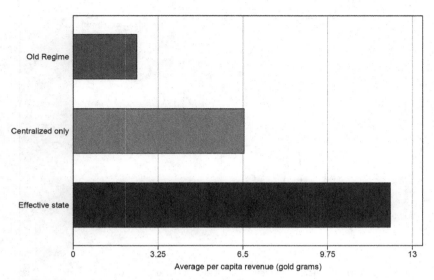

Figure 11 Regime Type and Per Capita Revenue in Europe,
1650–1913

Notes: Data are for 11 historical sovereign governments: Austria,
Belgium, Denmark, England, France, Dutch Republic/
Netherlands, Piedmont, Portugal, Prussia, Spain, and Sweden.
Total yearly observations: 1,502.

Sources: Dincecco (2011) and Dincecco, Federico, and Vindigni
(2011) for Piedmont.

capita revenue in England over 1650–1730. This period pre-dates
the economic sea change of the Industrial Revolution, which did
not begin until after 1750 (Mokyr, 2009: 80). Thus, we need not
worry about conflating the fiscal consequences of institutional

British, French, Danish, and other early modern empires cannot be depicted as
important for the construction of productive and viable fiscal systems for the
long-run growth of metropolitan economies. After meeting outlays for conquest
and the annual costs for the defense and governance of their colonized territories
and provinces, apart from an initial phase of plunder, such net flows probably
added rather small (even negative) amounts to the fiscal resources at the
disposal of metropolitan governments." Grafe and Irigoin (2006: 251–2) make
a similar point regarding the Spanish Empire. Huillery (2014) analyzes the fiscal
costs of French colonization to taxpayers in West Africa itself.

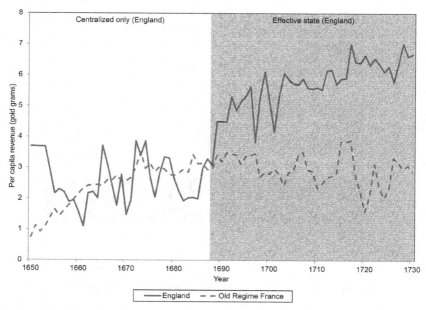

Figure 12 Regime Type and Per Capita Revenue in Pre-Industrial
England
Source: Dincecco (2011).

change with those of industrialization. English per capita revenue
grew by more than 80 percent between 1650 and 1730, while real
per capita GDP grew by less than 25 percent (Maddison, 2013).
This evidence suggests that fiscal improvements in England were
not just a function of economic development. Rather, institutional
change was important. Following the establishment of an effective
state in the aftermath of the Glorious Revolution of 1688 (as
described above), average English revenue was 5.68 gold grams
per capita: an increase of nearly 120 percent over the pre-1688
average.[23] To help show that this increase was not spurious,
Figure 12 includes a "placebo" revenue time series for Old

---

[23] The pre-effective-state average of 2.61 gold grams per capita pertains to the
1650–87 period, while the post-effective-state average pertains to the
1688–1730 period.

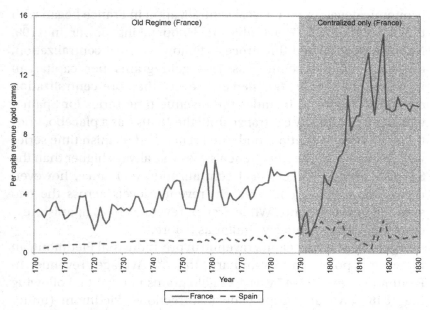

Figure 13 Regime Type and Per Capita Revenue in Pre-Industrial France
Source: Dincecco (2011).

Regime France, which was never an effective state over 1650–1730. Prior to 1688, both the English and French time series hovered between 1 and 4 gold grams per capita. After the establishment of an effective state in England, by contrast, the two times series diverged. There was a clear upward trend in English revenue levels, while French revenue levels were relatively similar as before.

The Industrial Revolution did not take place in Continental Europe until after 1870 (Mokyr, 1998). To further show that economic growth alone cannot explain greater revenue extraction, Figure 13 plots per capita revenue in pre-industrial France. Over 1700–1830, French per capita revenue grew by more than 160 percent, but real per capita GDP grew by less than 20 percent (Maddison, 2013). Thus, fiscal improvements in pre-industrial France do not appear to have simply been a consequence of economic development. Fiscal centralization in France began with the Revolution of 1789 (Table 3). Upon taking power in 1799, Napoleon completed this process. Following fiscal centralization, average French revenue was 7.82 gold grams per capita: an increase of nearly 80 percent over the pre-centralization average.[24] Figure 13 includes the revenue time series for Spain – which did not fiscally centralize until the 1840s – as a placebo. Prior to the French Revolution, both the French and Spanish time series were relatively stable (the French series was always higher than the Spanish series).[25] After fiscal centralization in France, however, there was a clear trend break in revenue levels across the two sovereign governments. While French revenues rose, Spanish revenues remained relatively similar as before.

Figure 14 plots per capita revenue in pre-industrial Piedmont, an important polity in pre-unitary Italy.[26] Average revenue in Piedmont over 1825–47 was 4.27 gold grams per capita. Following the 1848 wave of Europe-wide insurrections, Piedmont (under King Vittorio Emanuele II) became the only pre-unitary polity in Italy to uphold parliamentary government (Dincecco, Federico, and Vindigni, 2011: 895). In the aftermath of the establishment of an effective state in Piedmont, average per capita revenue increased by 50 percent.[27] Figure 14 includes a "placebo" revenue time series for the Kingdom of the Two Sicilies, another major pre-unitary polity in Italy. Unlike Piedmont, the Two Sicilies never became an effective state (Dincecco, Federico, and Vindigni,

[24] The post-centralization average pertains to the 1790–1830 period, while the pre-centralization average pertains to the 1700–89 period.

[25] Drelichman and Voth (2014: 263–9) argue that silver revenue from the Americas were in part to blame for low revenue under the Old Regime in Spain, because they reduced the Crown's incentive to undertake institutional reforms that would increase domestic fiscal capacity.

[26] Italy did not become a single sovereign political unit – the Kingdom of Italy, a constitutional monarchy – until 1861 (Dincecco, 2010: 309–11; Dincecco, Federico, and Vindigni, 2011: 896).

[27] The pre-effective-state average pertains to the 1825–47 period, while the post-effective-state average of 6.41 gold grams per capita pertains to the 1848–58 period.

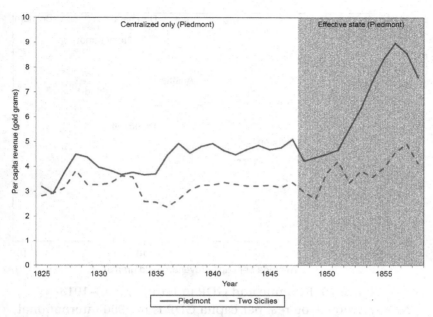

Figure 14 Regime Type and Per Capita Revenue in Pre-Industrial
Piedmont
Source: Dincecco, Federico, and Vindigni (2011).

2011: 895). Both revenue series were relatively stable prior to 1848,
hovering between 2 and 5 gold grams per capita (the revenue series
for Piedmont was always higher than that for the Two Sicilies).
The two series diverged, however, after institutional change in
Piedmont. Over the 1850s, revenue levels in Piedmont rose at
a notably faster rate than in the Two Sicilies.

3.2.4 Economic Implications

By enabling historical sovereign governments to provide basic
public goods including the rules of the game – law and order,
private property rights protections, and military defense – along
with the establishment of competitive and free domestic markets
(as described in Subsection 1.2), effective statehood could promote

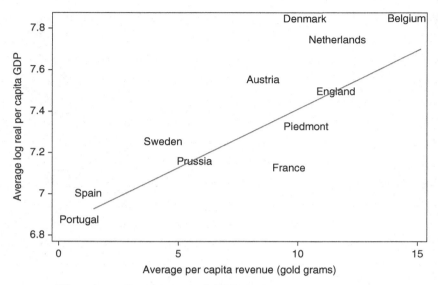

Figure 15 Revenue and GDP in Europe, 1650–1913
Notes: Average log real per capita GDP is in 1990 international
Geary-Khamis dollars. Data are averaged over 1650–1913.
Sources: Maddison (2013) for GDP and Dincecco (2011) and
Dincecco, Federico, and Vindigni (2011) for revenue.

subsequent economic development. Consistent with this view, the correlation between the state's ability to extract revenue and per capita GDP was strongly positive (Figure 15). Furthermore, average real per capita GDP under effective states (Conditions 1 and 2) was 2,162 dollars, more than double the average under the Old Regime (Figure 16).

Dincecco and Katz (2016) show econometric evidence for a significant relationship between national-level fiscal reforms and economic growth in Western Europe from the Old Regime to World War I. They control for polity fixed effects, common time trends, polity-specific time trends, and time-varying observables including external and internal military conflicts, population growth, and past GDP growth and levels. Their results suggest that extractive capacity improvements can explain roughly

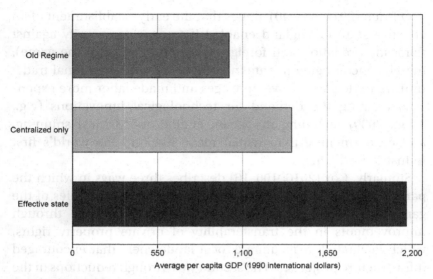

Figure 16 Regime Type and Per Capita GDP in Europe, 1650–1913
Notes: Data are for 11 historical sovereign governments: Austria,
Belgium, Denmark, England, France, Dutch Republic/
Netherlands, Piedmont, Portugal, Prussia, Spain, and Sweden.
Total yearly observations: 1,502.
Source: Maddison (2013).

one-half of the difference in average annual per capita GDP growth
rates over the 1700s between rivals England and France.
To account for reverse causation from economic growth to fiscal
reforms (beyond the sorts of controls described above), the authors
perform (i) a pulse dummy analysis, which displays no evidence of
pre-reform "anticipatory" effects, and (ii) a placebo analysis,
whereby the placebo coefficients for fiscal centralization are
small and not significant (unlike the actual coefficients, which
are both sizeable and significant).[28]

---

[28] A contemporary analog to the argument that economic development promotes
institutional reforms is known as the modernization hypothesis. According to
this argument, higher per capita income causes democratization (e.g., Lipset,
1959: 80). This hypothesis has been subject to vigorous debate (e.g., Barro,

O'Brien (2011: 436–40) argues that the early establishment of an effective state in England enabled it to provide security against domestic predation and foreign threats (i.e., rules of the game), thereby encouraging private investments and international trade. In turn, trade gains drove up wages and made labor more expensive, creating the demand for technological innovations (e.g., Allen, 2009) including the steam engine, mechanical spinning, and coke smelting that helped make England the world's first industrialized nation.

Similarly, Cox (2016: 100–16) describes three ways in which the parliamentary reform of 1688 in England remade the rules of the game and promoted industrialization. The first was through improvements in the transferability of private property rights, which facilitated deals among local landowners that encouraged infrastructure projects.[29] The second was through reductions in the negative external economic effects of political rent-seeking behavior, due to greater transparency in state deal-making via parliamentary acts (versus private favors granted by the Crown). The third was through the high and persistent demand by the effective English state (versus say the far less effective French state) for new military technology over the 1700s. Such high demand promoted technological innovations across several key military sectors including agriculture (for military rations), metallurgy (for weapons and the navy), textiles (for military uniforms), and transportation (for the shipment of government goods).

Rosenthal (1992: 100–21) argues that centralizing reforms in the aftermath of the Revolution of 1789 resolved local free-riding problems and increased agricultural productivity in France. His

1999; Hall and Jones, 1999; Przeworski et al., 2000; Boix and Stokes, 2003; Glaeser et al., 2004; Boix, 2011). Recently, scholars have provided new econometric evidence in support of the argument that the causal logic runs from democratic reforms to economic growth, and not vice versa (Acemoglu et al. 2008; Papaioannou and Siourounis, 2008; Acemoglu et al. 2015).

[29] Bogart (2011) shows evidence that average yearly investments in English roads and rivers in the six decades after the Glorious Revolution were nearly four times larger than in prior decades.

argument is similar in spirit to the first channel described by Cox (2016: 100–16) above. Under the Old Regime, property rights over eminent domain were divided between several local actors. Thus, large-scale irrigation projects were very costly, because different local groups could extract rents. The French Revolution granted the national government the ability to implement a uniform legal regime throughout France, improving the rules of the game. In turn, local actors could no longer hold up otherwise attractive large-scale irrigation projects. Litigation costs and delays fell, and irrigation became widespread. Between 1820 and 1865, for example, the irrigated area in Provence more than doubled.

Acemoglu et al. (2011) analyze the economic consequences of the institutional reforms undertaken by the post-revolutionary French government and Napoleon in the parts of Germany that France invaded between 1792 and 1815. Major institutional reforms included the implementation of the French civil legal code, the abolition of local guilds, and the establishment of equality before the law. German states may have undertaken "pre-emptive" institutional reforms in response to French military threats. To address this endogeneity concern, the authors instrument for the effects of institutional reforms on economic performance, exploiting the length of French occupation. Their econometric results indicate that German states that underwent Revolution-era reforms saw faster economic growth over the latter half of the 1800s. The authors attribute this result to the role that such reforms played in the establishment of market infrastructure (e.g., rules of the game, competitive and free domestic markets) that promoted private investments and technological innovations. This argument is akin to O'Brien's (2011: 436–40) argument as described above.[30]

---

[30] A related literature analyzes the long-run economic effects of historical institutional investments. Bockstette, Chanda, and Putterman (2002) construct a global state antiquity index that spans the dawn of the first millennium to the mid-twentieth century. They find a positive correlation between historical statehood and modern-day economic development. Dincecco and Prado (2012) document a positive relationship between fiscal capacity and economic

3.3 Rise of the Welfare State

In the previous subsection, I have argued that Conditions 1 and 2 were satisfied and effective national-level states were thereby established in Western Europe by the mid-nineteenth century. Such states could not only gather enough revenue to accomplish their intended policy actions, but were more likely to spend funds on basic public goods (e.g., rules of the game) that supported market-oriented economic development (versus wasteful spending). In this section, I analyze the third and final key inflection point in long-run state development in Western Europe: the rise of welfare states.

3.3.1 Social Spending, Redistributive Taxation, and Inequality

Social Spending

The stylized evidence supports the view that effective statehood at the national level was the institutional bedrock upon which twentieth-century welfare states were built. Table 6 shows the historical evolution of social spending – the ratio of national government spending on housing, healthcare, retirement, unemployment compensation, and family assistance to GDP – for sample nations in Western Europe across four benchmark years between 1880 and 1990 according to Lindert (2004: 12–13). Through 1930, social spending was very low or non-existent, averaging less than

performance today. To instrument for current fiscal capacity (which may be endogenous to economic development levels), they exploit historical war casualties, which proxy for past fiscal investments (Tilly, 1992: 67–95; Besley and Persson, 2011: 40–102). Acharya and Lee (2016) construct data on succession disputes in medieval Europe, which they argue turned violent, reducing the prospects for subsequent state development. They show evidence that European regions with historical shortages of male heirs are relatively poor today. Cassidy, Dincecco, and Onorato (2017) analyze the relationship between historical warfare and modern-day economic development at the regional level in Europe. They argue that historical warfare promoted local economic development over time, because urban centers were safe harbors from conflict threats.

Table 6 Social Spending (Percent) in Europe, 1880–1990

	1880	1930	1960	1990
Austria	0	1	16	25
Belgium	0	1	13	23
Denmark	1	3	12	27
France	0	1	13	24
Germany	1	5	18	20
Italy	0	0	13	21
Netherlands	0	1	12	28
Portugal	0	0	–	13
Spain	0	0	–	17
Sweden	1	3	11	32
United Kingdom	1	2	10	18

Notes: Social spending is the ratio of national government spending on housing, healthcare, retirement, unemployment compensation, and family assistance to GDP.
Source: Lindert (2004: 12–13).

2 percent of GDP among sample nations.[31] From World War II onward, by contrast, social spending soared (Lindert, 2004: 11). I will examine the role of warfare in greater detail ahead. By 1960, social spending averaged 13 percent across sample nations. By 1990, this average was more than 20 percent.

---

[31] To be fair, the focus on social spending by national governments overlooks pre-twentieth-century efforts by local governments to provide public goods. For example, Greif and Iyigun (2013) analyze the role of county-level poor relief in early modern England, which they argue reduced political violence and promoted technological innovations. Guinnane and Streb (2011) study the role of local organizations through which miners could protect themselves against accidents and sickness in nineteenth-century Germany. Kesztenbaum and Rosenthal (2017) evaluate the relationship between sanitation infrastructure improvements and mortality across neighborhoods in nineteenth-century Paris, while Chapman (2017) evaluates this relationship across towns in nineteenth-century England. Nafziger (2011) analyzes the effect of local representative political institutions on primary education outcomes in nineteenth-century Russia.

Table 7 Establishment of Income Taxation in Europe prior to World War II

United Kingdom	1842
Austria	1849
Italy	1864
Netherlands	1893
Sweden	1902
Denmark	1903
France	1911
Germany	1920
Belgium	1922
Portugal	--
Spain	--

Notes: The year column refers to the year in which the national government introduced the permanent personal income tax.
Source: Aidt and Jensen (2009: 162).

Income Taxation

The historical shift in taxation patterns from indirect taxation on customs and excises to direct taxation on income and wealth helped undergird greater social spending (Lindert, 2004: 302–5; Besley and Persson, 2013: 56–8). This shift from narrow to broad tax policy reduced both the administrative and incentive costs of taxation (Lindert, 2004: 302–5). Table 7 dates the establishment of the permanent personal income tax across sovereign governments in Western Europe according to Aidt and Jensen (2009: 162). The United Kingdom was the first to implement the permanent income tax in 1842. By the start of World War I in 1914, 7 out of 11 sample governments had established the income tax. Belgium and Germany, moreover, implemented the income tax in the early 1920s.

Figure 17 plots the historical evolution of the average top marginal income tax rate between 1900 and 2010 according to Scheve and Stasavage (2016) for a similar sample as above.[32]

[32] Scheve and Stasavage (2016) do not provide marginal income tax rate data for Portugal.

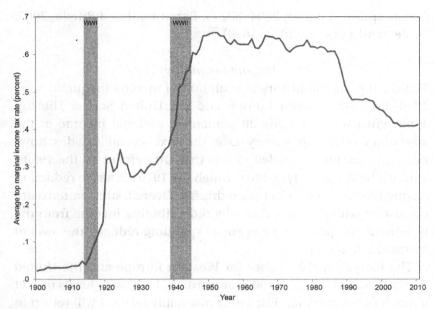

Figure 17 Evolution of Top Rate of Income Taxation in Europe, 1900–2010

Notes: Average top marginal income tax rate is the yearly top marginal income tax rate averaged over 10 Western European nations. The included nations are Austria, Belgium, Denmark, France, Germany, Italy, Netherlands, Spain, Sweden, and the United Kingdom.

Source: Scheve and Stasavage (2016).

Consistent with the view that greater direct taxation helped undergird higher social spending, the average top marginal income tax rate rose from well under 10 percent at the start of the twentieth century to more than 60 percent by 1950, where it held steady for the next two decades. Sharp increases during World Wars I and II punctuated this rise. From the 1970s onward, the average top marginal income tax rate fell, in part because sample nations shifted toward value-added taxation on consumption (Lindert, 2004: 302–5; Beramendi and Rueda, 2007; Besley and Persson, 2013: 56–8).[33]

Income Inequality

Figure 18 plots the historical evolution of income inequality over 1910–2010 for Western Europe and the United States. The top 1 percent earned roughly 20 percent of national income at the start of the twentieth century. Over the next several decades, however, income inequality fell to less than 10 percent by the 1950s, where it held relatively stable through the 1970s. A sharp reduction during World War II punctuated this fall. Overall, such patterns are consistent with the view that – by redistributing income from the wealthy to the poor – greater social spending reduced the level of inequality in society.

The inequality time series for Western Europe and the United States diverged from the 1980s onward. US inequality levels rose at a much faster rate than European inequality levels. I will return to this divergence ahead.

3.3.2 Role of Mass Warfare

To explain the dramatic fall in inequality over the first part of the twentieth century, Scheve and Stasavage (2010, 2012, 2016: 19–22) highlight the role of mass warfare.[34] Their argument runs as follows. The scale of World Wars I and II was unprecedented, drawing recruits from large portions of national populations. To help achieve social consensus in favor of such huge war efforts, it was important to promote equal burden-sharing among different groups in society. The richest individuals were the least likely to fight, due to deferments, exemptions, or old age. Such individuals

---

[33] The evolution of the average top marginal inheritance tax rate over the twentieth century is similar to that of the average top marginal income tax rate (Scheve and Stasavage, 2016: 10).

[34] Similarly, Piketty's (2014: 237, 274–6) explanation for twentieth-century reductions in income inequality emphasizes the role of the two World Wars and the public policy decisions that flowed from them (e.g., high income taxation). Also see Milanovic (2016: 480–1) and Scheidel (2017: 130–74).

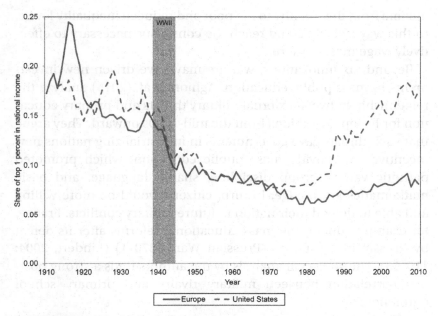

Figure 18 Evolution of Income Inequality: Europe versus the
United States, 1910–2010

Notes: Share of top 1 percent in national income is the share of
pre-tax income earned by individuals at the top 1 percent of the
income distribution averaged over 10 Western European nations.
The included nations are Austria, Belgium, Denmark, France,
Germany, Italy, Netherlands, Spain, Sweden, and the United
Kingdom.
Source: World Top Incomes Database (as reported by Scheve and
Stasavage, 2016).

could also potentially profit from wartime demands for products
made by their firms. To attain more equal burden-sharing in
wartime, therefore, the government "conscripted" the income
and wealth of rich individuals through greater direct taxation.[35]
New revenue could be spent on social programs that redistributed

---

[35] In a somewhat similar manner, Aidt and Jensen (2013) show evidence for
a positive relationship between warfare and government size in Western
Europe over 1820–1913.

income from the wealthy to the poor and reduced inequality levels. In this way, society could reach the consensus necessary to effectively wage mass warfare.[36]

Beyond tax innovations, warfare may have driven new investments in mass public education. Aghion et al. (2015) analyze the relationship between external military threats and primary education for European nations from the mid-1800s onward. They argue that such threats gave governments in industrializing nations new incentives to provide mass public education, which promoted patriotic values, group discipline, shared language, and basic mathematics knowledge. In turn, citizens would be more willing and able to defend their nation in future military conflicts. France, for example, undertook mass educational reforms after its defeat by Prussia in the Franco-Prussian War (1870–1) (Lindert, 2004: 110–13). The statistical analysis by the authors finds a strong positive correlation between military rivalry and primary school enrollment.

3.3.3　Role of Social Conflict

The discussion in the previous subsection focuses on external factors – namely, mass warfare and military threats – that help explain the growth of welfare states over the twentieth century. Yet I must also highlight the potential importance of domestic factors. Acemoglu and Robinson (2000, 2006: 23–30) focus on the role of revolutionary threats by the (relatively poor) citizen majority. They argue that, under non-democracy, traditional elites have formal or de jure political power, which they can use to curb income redistribution. The citizen majority, however, has informal or de facto political power, due to strength in numbers. A threat of revolution by the citizen majority to overthrow the non-democracy and establish democracy is one way that they can transform their de facto power into de jure power and secure greater income

---

[36] Lindert (2004: 179–82) argues that the extension of voting rights to broad swaths of society help explain the rise in redistributive spending in Western Europe over 1880–1930. However, Scheve and Stasavage (2016: 125–7) find no such effect.

redistribution in their favor. To prevent the revolutionary threat from turning into actual revolution, which may be very costly in terms of property loss, traditional elites may be willing to yield de jure political power to the citizen majority through democratization (depending on the relative costs of repression). Democratic reform is more credible than a mere promise to increase future income redistribution, because traditional elites may change their minds once the revolutionary threat subsides. Aidt and Jensen (2009) find statistical support for the revolutionary threat argument for a sample of 20-plus European nations between 1820 and 1938.

Ansell and Samuels (2014: 9–14) highlight the role of intra-elite conflict between the (economically ascendant) middle class and traditional elites. In contrast to Acemoglu and Robinson (2006), they argue that democratization derives from a threat of predation "from above" by traditional elites, rather than a threat of revolution "from below" by the poor. Namely, under non-democracy, the middle class fears that traditional elites will attempt to exploit de jure political power and predate upon their newly held wealth. To reduce this risk, the middle class demands de jure political representation through democratic reform. The authors argue that democratization is most likely to occur when land inequality is low and income inequality is high. Low land inequality favors democratic reform because it suggests that there are too few large landowners to enforce a traditional agricultural policy of low wages and low labor mobility. Similarly, high income inequality favors democratic reform because it signals the economic rise of the middle class. As this disenfranchised group earns a larger portion of national income, it becomes more likely to demand de jure political representation. Ansell and Samuels (2014: 95–123) show statistical evidence in support of the elite competition argument for a worldwide database over 1820–2004.[37]

---

[37] Several other recent works analyze the relationship between domestic factors and fiscal development in nineteenth- and twentieth-century Europe. Beramendi and Queralt (2016) highlight the role of political myopia. They argue that short-run political incentives swayed both conservatives and liberal elites to extend the voting franchise to wider swaths of society. Over time,

3.3.4 Economic Implications

The three subsections above document the historical evolution of the welfare state over the twentieth century, and discuss the potential roles of external and domestic factors. I have described the different theoretical ways in which social spending and inequality levels may influence economic outcomes in Subsection 1.2. The empirical evidence regarding such relationships is not clear-cut.[38] I focus here on the results of two recent wide-ranging analyses. The first analysis is by Lindert (2004), who evaluates the relationship between social spending and economic development in OECD nations from the late eighteenth century to the present day. A main finding of his inquiry is that the net loss in per capita GDP due to social spending is trivial over time. Put differently, greater social spending does not appear to be detrimental to long-run economic development. The second analysis is by Ostry, Berg, and Tsangarides (2014), who evaluate the economic effects of inequality and redistribution across more than 170 nations over four decades. Their statistical analysis shows evidence that (i) redistribution is not typically associated with negative economic growth and (ii) lower inequality is associated with faster and more sustained economic growth (holding the level of

---

however, such choices were sub-optimal for elites, because their tax burdens grew (given greater income redistribution). Beramendi, Dincecco, and Rogers (2016) argue that capitalist elites – unlike traditional agricultural elites – may have preferred to invest in greater fiscal capacity (via greater direct taxation on themselves) in order to provide a higher amount of public goods such as transportation infrastructure that improved economic productivity in an industrializing society. Their argument draws on Lizzeri and Persico (2004). Mares and Queralt (2015), by contrast, analyze the incentive of traditional agricultural elites themselves to establish income taxation. They argue that the income tax shifted the tax burden toward capitalist elites, thereby counteracting the loss of economic power by agricultural elites due to industrialization. Finally, Queralt (2015) evaluates the relationship between fiscal capacity levels and trade policy. He argues that mercantilism helped promote early state-building. Once fiscal capacity improved enough, however, mercantilism was abandoned in favor of free trade.

[38] Ostry, Berg, and Tsangarides (2014: 7–11) provide a recent review of the relevant empirical literature.

redistribution constant). Ostry, Berg, and Tsangarides conclude that the trade-off between redistribution and growth does not generally appear to be large. This conclusion is similar in spirit to Lindert's result as described above.

3.3.5 Politics and Inequality

To wrap up this subsection, I briefly return to the historical evolution of income inequality in Western Europe and the United States as described in Figure 18. Recall that the two inequality time series evolved in a similar manner until the 1980s, when there was a clear divergence. Namely, post-1980 inequality levels rose much more rapidly in the United States than in Western Europe, even though productivity and technology developments were similar across both regions (Alvaredo et al., 2013: 5). To help explain this divergence, Alvaredo et al. (2013: 7–9) focus on post-1980 policy differences between Western Europe and the United States. They argue that one key explanatory factor concerns differences in income tax policy. From the early 1930s to the early 1980s, top income tax rates in the United States were above 60 percent (Alvaredo et al., 2013: 7). By 2010, however, this rate was less than half of its 1950 value (Alvaredo et al., 2013: 7). In Germany and France, by contrast, post-1980 reductions in the top income tax rate were notably less severe than in the United States (Alvaredo et al., 2013: 7). The authors find a striking relationship between changes in income tax rates and income inequality. Since 1960, for example, the top income tax rate in the United States fell by nearly 50 percentage points, while the (pre-tax) income share of the top 1 percent rose by 10 percentage points (Alvaredo et al., 2013: 7–8). In Germany, however, there was no major reduction in the top income tax rate over this period, and no increase in the income share of the top 1 percent (Alvaredo et al., 2013: 7–8). Overall, this evidence lends further support to the view that deliberate policy decisions – and not just productivity and technological trends – play an important role in how inequality levels in society evolve over time (Alvaredo et al., 2013: 4–6; Milanovic, 2016: 481–2).

4 Why Europe?

The previous section analyzes long-run state development in Western Europe from the medieval era to the twentieth century. To conclude this inquiry, I now briefly study the European state development experience in comparative perspective. The purpose of this analysis is to sharpen our understanding of the historical features that may have helped make Western Europe different.

Rigorous study of the long-run process of state development in world regions beyond Europe is a key area for future research. What follows is just one step in this direction. I highlight recent research that shares this important goal throughout this section.

4.1 Historical Snapshot

Figure 19 provides a snapshot of historical differences in extractive capacity across a sampling of sovereign governments in Eurasia. In the decade prior to the French Revolution, average revenue was highest in England, at more than 11 gold grams per capita. This amount was more than double that of rival France. Still, both Western European nations gathered a great deal more revenue per capita than sovereign governments in other parts of Eurasia. In Russia, average per capita revenue over the 1780s was less than 2 gold grams. In China, India, and the Ottoman Empire, this average was less than 1 gold gram.[39]

The stylized evidence above suggests that historical state capacity in Western Europe was high relative to other parts of the world. To help explain why, I again draw on the conceptual framework from Section 2. I contrast two "Old World" regions that are economically and geographically diverse from Western Europe, yet are relatively similar in terms of physical size: China and sub-Saharan Africa.[40]

---

[39] Karaman and Pamuk (2010: 611), Hoffman (2015b: 51), and Gupta, Ma, and Roy (2016: 57–9) also show evidence that historical extractive capacity was much greater in Western Europe than elsewhere in Eurasia.

[40] This comparative analysis draws on Dincecco and Onorato (2017: chapter 6).

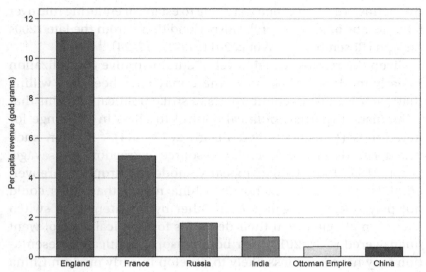

Figure 19 Per Capita Revenue across Eurasia, 1780s
Notes: Data for England, France, the Ottoman Empire, and
Russia are the 1780–89 average, according to the Karaman and
Pamuk (2010) database, which provides revenue data in both gold
and silver currency units. I use gold units for consistency with other
parts of this inquiry's analysis. Data for China are for 1776 (revenue
under central government control), according to Hoffman (2015b:
51). Data for India are for circa 1800, according to Gupta, Ma, and
Roy (2016: 57). The original data for China and India are in silver
units. To convert them into gold units, I first calculated the average
silver-to-gold exchange rate for the five states listed above,
according to Karaman and Pamuk (2010), and then divided the
original data in silver units by this rate.
Sources: Karaman and Pamuk (2010), Hoffman (2015b: 51), and
Gupta, Ma, and Roy (2016: 57).

4.2 Comparative Perspective

4.2.1 Early Modern China

Local institutional fragmentation within territorial states in medieval
Europe was typically high and long-lasting (see Subsection 3.1).

By contrast, rulers in China were able to establish enduring rule over large swaths of territory and satisfy Condition 1 from the late 1200s onward (Rosenthal and Wong, 2011: 12–13, 17–24).[41]

Given the relatively high level of administrative centralization in early modern China, rulers there may have been less willing than their European counterparts to strike political bargains that relinquished (partial) political control to elites in exchange for new funds (Blockmans and t'Hart, 2013: 434).[42] Rather, such rulers could rely on coercive resource extraction (Stasavage, 2016b: 155, 159). Unlike in early modern Europe, moreover, administrative centralization in China meant that elites could not play rulers off against each other by threatening to switch sovereign allegiances if their demands for political control went unanswered (Cox, 2017). For both reasons, political representation may have been less likely to develop in early modern China than in Europe. Put differently, the lack of enduring political fragmentation in early modern China may have made it less likely that institutional checks on ruler power (Sub-condition 2a) would emerge, obstructing further state development. This institutional difference may help explain why historical extractive capacity was so much lower in early modern China than in England or France (Figure 19).

Beyond the absence of effective ruler checks, other features may help explain the relatively low level of extractive capacity in early modern China. Sng and Moriguchi (2014) focus on the problem of geographical scale. Given China's large size, it was very difficult for

---

[41] Liu (2015) analyzes state development in China over 960–1279.

[42] Early modern China did in fact participate in military conflicts. According to Hoffman (2015b: 70–1), China fought interstate wars in more than 50 percent of all years over 1500–1800, though more than 95 percent of them were against Steppe nomads. Ko, Koyama, and Sng (2014) and Gupta, Ma, and Roy (2016) relate different types of military threats (multi-directional versus unidirectional, or external versus internal) to state capacity differences in early modern China and Europe. Kiser and Cai (2003) and Hui (2005) study the relationship between warfare and state development in ancient China relative to early modern Europe. Ferejohn and Rosenbluth (2010) analyze this relationship in medieval Japan, a historical rival of China.

the ruler to monitor tax bureaucrats. Tax extortion by bureaucrats, however, would anger taxpayers and threaten regime stability. To prevent this outcome, the ruler found it optimal to keep taxation low. Ma and Rubin (2016) analyze another potential ruler incentive to maintain a weak tax administration. By restricting the state's ability to monitor tax bureaucrats, weak institutions allowed such individuals to hide bribes, encouraging their loyalty to the regime and thereby promoting stability.[43]

4.2.2 Pre-Colonial Sub-Saharan Africa

Pre-colonial sub-Saharan Africa was ethnically and politically fragmented (Thornton, 1999: 3–4; Herbst, 2000: 44).[44] In this respect, it did not appear to differ greatly from early modern Europe. One historical feature that did in fact distinguish pre-colonial sub-Saharan Africa from early modern Europe (and China), however, was the land/labor ratio. In 1500, there were only 2 people per square kilometer in sub-Saharan Africa, but more than 10 people per square kilometer in Europe (and China) (Herbst, 2000: 16).

Herbst (2000: 35–57) argues that the high land/labor ratio in pre-colonial sub-Saharan Africa meant that state power was non-territorial in nature. In early modern Europe, territory was relatively scarce, making it a valuable resource to fight over (Hale, 1985: 22–3). In pre-colonial sub-Saharan Africa, by contrast, control over territory often went unchallenged, since the costs for individuals to migrate to virgin land in response to territorial threats were so low

[43] Ang (2016) and Lu, Luan, and Sng (2016) analyze the relationship between state development and economic growth in twentieth-century China, while Johnson (1982), Amsden (1989), Wade (1990), and Evans (1995) evaluate contemporary state-led development programs in neighbors Japan, South Korea, and Taiwan.

[44] Furthermore, warfare was common in this context (e.g., Thornton, 1999: 1–18; Reid, 2012: 1–17). Osafo-Kwaako and Robinson (2013) analyze the relationship between warfare and state development in pre-colonial Sub-Saharan Africa. Bates (2014) and Reid (2014) evaluate this relationship in the face of the European colonial experience over the 1800s, while Thies (2007) evaluates it over the late twentieth century. Besley and Querol-Reynal (2014) analyze the long-run relationship between pre-colonial warfare and contemporary civil conflict in Africa.

(Herbst, 2000: 39–40). It was thus very difficult for sovereign governments to satisfy Condition 1 and establish both the political authority and the administrative ability to rule over relatively large swaths of territory (Herbst, 2000: 39–40).[45] Put differently, the high land/labor ratio may have made it less likely that historical institutional centralization at the "national level" would occur in sub-Saharan Africa, thwarting further state development.[46]

Major historical events such as the transatlantic slave trade may have further reduced the state's ability to broadcast institutional power in sub-Saharan Africa. Whatley and Gillezeau (2011), for example, argue that the transatlantic slave trade weakened the incentive of African rulers to make political bargains with social groups over local policy concessions in exchange for greater revenue (as in early modern Europe), because such individuals were more valuable as potential slaves than as potential taxpayers. They show evidence that the transatlantic slave trade generated an increase in the amount of small and independent villages, exacerbating ethnic divisions.[47]

---

[45] According to Thornton (1999: 3–4), for example, more than half of all individuals in early modern Atlantic Africa lived in states that were just 50 kilometers wide, roughly equivalent in size to a modern-day US county. Fenske (2013) analyzes the long-run economic and political consequences of the high historical land/labor ratio in Africa. Bates (1983: 41–2) highlights a political benefit of such land abundance. Due to the low historical costs of exit, individuals were in a strong bargaining position vis-à-vis rulers, which they could exploit in favor of relatively egalitarian policy outcomes (Sub-condition 2a).

[46] Gennaioli and Rainer (2007) and Michalopoulos and Papaioannou (2013) document a positive relationship between the extent of pre-colonial state centralization (when it did in fact occur) and modern-day economic and political performance in Africa. Similarly, Depetris-Chauvin (2014) shows evidence that greater historical state centralization reduces contemporary civil conflicts in Sub-Saharan Africa. Beyond state centralization, Moscona, Nunn, and Robinson (2017) highlight the long-run importance of historical social structures such as segmentary lineage in Africa.

[47] Nunn (2008) finds a negative relationship between historical slave trades and contemporary economic development in Africa, which Nunn and Wantchekon (2011) attribute to a long-standing culture of mistrust that the slave trades helped create. Fenske and Kala (2017) analyze the consequences of the 1807 Slave Trade Act for subsequent intra-African conflict.

Bates (2014) and Reid (2014) analyze the impact of European colonial efforts in the late 1800s on African state development. Both argue that the "imperial peace" implemented by European powers cut short an indigenous process of war-related state development in Africa.[48] In a similar manner, Bates (2010: 57–66) argues that Cold War-era foreign aid hampered African political development by reducing the incentive of rulers to seek domestic political consensus for their policy choices. Finally, García-Ponce and Wantchekon (2015) analyze the relationship between post–World War II independence movements and current political regime types in Africa. They argue that nations in which there were independence movements characterized by urban mass protest (versus rural insurgency) are more likely to be democratic today, because such movements promoted a culture of political inclusion and peaceful dissent.

4.2.3 Implications

The brief comparative analysis in the previous two subsections helps bring into focus the sorts of historical features that may have made the state development process in Western Europe unique. Two such features appear to stand out: the high level of political fragmentation and the low land/labor ratio. Relative to early modern China, high political fragmentation in Western Europe may have made it more likely that historical rulers would have the incentive to strike political bargains that granted (partial) political control to elites in exchange for new revenue. Relative to pre-colonial sub-Saharan Africa, the low land/labor ratio in Western Europe may have made it more likely that historical governments would (over time) gain both the political authority and the administrative ability to establish "national-level" institutional centralization.

---

[48] Recent quantitatively-oriented works on fiscal development in colonial Africa include Gardner (2012: 17–62), Frankema and van Waijenburg (2014), and Huillery (2014).

Beyond the high level of political fragmentation and the low land/labor ratio, other historical features may have also helped make long-run state development in Western Europe different. Centeno's (2002: 101–66) analysis of warfare and state-building in post-independence Latin America, for example, highlights the role of distributive politics (Sub-condition 2b). In contrast to early modern Europe, historical governments in Latin America could not overcome chronic intra-elite divisions due to regional allegiances, birth status (American versus Spanish), and power struggles between the church and the state (Centeno, 2002: 141–60). Furthermore, many Latin American elites preferred weak fiscal states that did not interfere with their ability to profit from natural resource extraction and the global commodity trade (Centeno, 1997: 1592–5).[49]

4.3   Toward a Global History of State Capacity

I view the brief comparative analysis in Subsection 4.2 as just one step in a research agenda that rigorously analyzes the process of long-run state development across the globe. I have highlighted above a wide range of recent works for China, sub-Saharan Africa, and Latin America that contribute to this important task. I look forward to new quantitatively oriented historical research for these regions, along with such research for other parts of today's

---

[49] Kurtz (2013) and Soifer (2015) are two recent book-length treatments on long-run state development in Latin America. Kurtz (2013) emphasizes the social origins of state-building, while Soifer (2015) highlights incentive structures within new state administrations. Arias (2013) and Garfias (2016) relate different types of (non-parliamentary) ruler-elite bargains to fiscal capacity improvements in late colonial Mexico. Summerhill (2015) examines why the state's credible commitment to debt repayment did not promote broader financial development in nineteenth-century Brazil. Thies (2005) evaluates the relationship between military rivalry and state development in Latin America over the twentieth century. Acemoglu, García-Jimeno, and Robinson (2015) analyze the effect of local state capacity investments on economic development in modern-day Colombia. Musacchio and Lazzarini (2014) study the state-led development program in late twentieth-century Brazil.

developing world, including India, the Middle East, and Southeast Asia.[50] In this way, we will further improve our understanding of both the historical origins of state capacity and the relationship between past state capacity investments and contemporary patterns of economic and political development.

---

[50] For example, Banerjee and Iyer (2005) analyze the relationship between colonial revenue institutions and modern-day economic performance at the district level in India. Roy (2013) and Gupta, Ma, and Roy (2016) evaluate the historical relationship between warfare and state development in the Indian context. Blaydes and Chaney (2013) argue that medieval political innovations promoted internal stability in Europe relative to the Middle East. Rubin (2017: 149–200) links the political importance of religion to the historical economic divergence between Europe and the Middle East. Slater (2010) is a recent book-length treatment on long-run state development in Southeast Asia. He highlights the role of country-level differences in historical patterns of mass political actions. Dell, Lane, and Querubin (2015) analyze the effect of historical state capacity investments on village-level economic development today in Vietnam. Pepinsky (2016) evaluates the relationship between informal colonial-era institutions and current local governance outcomes in Indonesia.

Works Cited

Abramson, S. and C. Boix (2015). "The Roots of the Industrial Revolution: Political Institutions or (Socially-Embedded) Know-How?" Working paper, Princeton University.

Acemoglu, D. (2005). "Politics and Economics in Weak and Strong States." *Journal of Monetary Economics*, 52: 1199–226.

Acemoglu, D. and J. Robinson (2000). "Why Did the West Extend the Franchise? Democracy, Inequality, and Growth in Historical Perspective." *Quarterly Journal of Economics*, 115: 1167–99.

Acemoglu, D., S. Johnson, and J. Robinson (2005). "Institutions as a Fundamental Cause of Long-Run Growth." In P. Aghion and S. Durlauf, eds., *Handbook of Economic Growth*, pp. 385–472, Amsterdam, Netherlands: Elsevier.

Acemoglu, D., S. Johnson, and J. Robinson (2005). "The Rise of Europe: Atlantic Trade, Institutional Change, and Economic Growth." *American Economic Review*, 94: 546–79.

Acemoglu, D. and J. Robinson (2006). *Economic Origins of Dictatorship and Democracy*. Cambridge, UK: Cambridge University Press.

Acemoglu, D., S. Johnson, J. Robinson, and P. Yared (2008). "Income and Democracy." *American Economic Review*, 98: 808–42.

Acemoglu, D., D. Cantoni, S. Johnson, and J. Robinson (2011). "The Consequences of Radical Reform: The French Revolution." *American Economic Review*, 101: 3286–307.

Acemoglu, D., D. Ticchi, and A. Vindigni (2011). "Emergence and Persistence of Inefficient States." *Journal of the European Economic Association*, 9: 177–208.

Acemoglu, D. and J. Robinson (2012). *Why Nations Fail*. London, UK: Profile.

Acemoglu, D., S. Naidu, P. Restrepo, and J. Robinson (2015). "Democracy Does Cause Growth." Working paper, Massachusetts Institute of Technology.

Acemoglu, D., C. García-Jimeno, and J. Robinson (2015) "State Capacity and Economic Development: A Network Approach." *American Economic Review*, 105: 2364–409.

Acemoglu, D., J. Moscona, and J. Robinson (2016) "State Capacity and American Technology: Evidence from the Nineteenth Century." *American Economic Review: Papers and Proceedings*, 106: 61–7.

Acemoglu, D., L. Fergusson, J. Robinson, D. Romero, and J. Vargas (2016). "The Perils of Top-Down State Building: Evidence from Colombia's False Positives." NBER working paper 22617.

Acemoglu, D., J. Robinson, and R. Torvik (2016). "The Political Agenda Effect and State Centralization." NBER working paper 22250.

Acharya, A. and A. Lee (2016). "Path Dependence in European Development: Medieval Politics, Conflict, and State-Building." Working paper, Stanford University.

Aghion, P., X. Jaravel, T. Persson, and D. Rouzet (2015). "Education and Military Rivalry." Working paper, Harvard University.

Aghion, P., U. Akcigit, J. Cagé, and W. Kerr (2016). "Taxation, Corruption, and Growth." NBER working paper 21928.

Aidt, T. and P. Jensen (2009). "The Taxman Tools Up: An Event History Study of the Introduction of the Personal Income Tax." *Journal of Public Economics*, 93: 160–75.

Aidt, T. and P. Jensen (2013). "Democratization and the Size of Government: Evidence from the Long Nineteenth Century." *Public Choice*, 157: 511–42.

Alesina, A. and R. Perotti (1996). "Income Distribution, Political Instability, and Investment." *European Economic Review*, 40: 1203–28.

Alesina, A, E. Glaeser, and B. Sacerdote (2001). "Why Doesn't the United States Have a European-Style Welfare State?" *Brookings Paper on Economics Activity*, 187–278.

Alesina, A. and E. Spolaore (2003). *The Size of Nations*. Cambridge, MA: MIT Press.

Allen, R. (2003). *From Farm to Factory*. Princeton, NJ: Princeton University Press.

Allen, R. (2009). *The British Industrial Revolution in Global Perspective*. Cambridge, UK: Cambridge University Press.

Alvaredo, F., A. Atkinson, T. Piketty, and E. Saez (2013). "The Top 1 Percent in International and Historical Perspective." *Journal of Economic Perspectives*, 27: 3–20.

Amsden, A. (1989). *Asia's Next Giant*. Oxford, UK: Oxford University Press.

Ang, Y.Y. (2016). *How China Escaped the Poverty Trap*. Ithaca, NY: Cornell University Press.

Ansell, B. and D. Samuels (2014). *Inequality and Democratization.* Cambridge, UK: Cambridge University Press.

Arias, L. (2013). "Building Fiscal Capacity in Colonial Mexico: From Fragmentation to Centralization." *Journal of Economic History*, 73: 662–93.

Bairoch, P. (1988). *Cities and Economic Development.* Chicago, IL: University of Chicago Press.

Banerjee, A. and L. Iyer (2005). "History, Institutions, and Economic Performance: The Legacy of Colonial Land Tenure Systems in India." *American Economic Review*, 95: 1190–213.

Bardhan, P. (2016). "State and Development: The Need for a Reappraisal of the Current Literature." *Journal of Economic Literature*, 54: 862–92.

Barro, R. (1999). "Determinants of Democracy." *Journal of Political Economy*, 107: 158–83.

Barro, R. (2000). "Inequality and Growth in a Panel of Countries." *Journal of Economic Growth*, 5: 5–32.

Bates, R. (1983). *Essays on the Political Economy of Africa.* Berkeley, CA: University of California Press.

Bates, R. (2010). *Prosperity and Violence* (Second Edition). New York, NY: Norton.

Bates, R. (2014). "The Imperial Peace." In E. Akyeampong, R. Bates, N. Nunn, and J. Robinson, eds., *Africa's Development in Historical Perspective*, pp. 424–46, Cambridge, UK: Cambridge University Press.

Bates, R. and D.H. Lien (1985). "A Note on Taxation, Development, and Representative Government." *Politics & Society*, 14: 53–70.

Benabou, R. (2000). "Unequal Societies: Income Distribution and the Social Contract." *American Economic Review*, 90: 96–129.

Beramendi, P. and D. Rueda (2007). "Social Democracy Constrained: Indirect Taxation in Industrialized Democracies." *British Journal of Political Science*, 37: 619–41.

Beramendi, P., M. Dincecco, and M. Rogers (2016). "Intra-Elite Competition and Long-Run Fiscal Development." Working paper, Duke University.

Beramendi, P. and D. Queralt (2016). "The Electoral Origins of the Fiscal State." Working paper, Duke University.

Besley, T. and M. Kudamatsu (2008). "Making Autocracy Work." In E. Helpman, ed., *Institutions and Economic Performance*, pp. 452–510, Cambridge, MA: Harvard University Press.

Besley, T. and T. Persson (2011). *The Pillars of Prosperity*. Princeton, NJ: Princeton University Press.

Besley, T. and T. Persson (2013). "Taxation and Development." In A. Auerbach, R. Chetty, M. Feldstein, and E. Saez, eds., *Handbook of Public Economics*, pp. 51–110, Amsterdam, Netherlands: Elsevier.

Besley, T. and M. Reynal-Querol (2014). "The Legacy of Historical Conflict: Evidence from Africa." *American Political Science Review*, 108: 319–36.

Blattman, C. and E. Miguel (2010). "Civil War." *Journal of Economic Literature*, 48: 3–57.

Blaydes, L. and E. Chaney (2013). "The Feudal Revolution and Europe's Rise: Political Divergence of the Christian West and the Muslim World Before 1500 CE." *American Political Science Review*, 107: 16–34.

Bleakley, H. and J. Lin (2015). "History and the Sizes of Cities." *American Economic Review: Papers and Proceedings*, 105: 558–63.

Blockmans, W. (1989). "Voracious States and Obstructing Cities: An Aspect of State Formation in Pre-Industrial Europe." *Theory and Society*, 18: 733–55.

Blockmans, W. (1998). "Representation (Since the Thirteenth Century)." In R. McKitterick, ed., *The New Cambridge Medieval History*, pp. 29–64, Cambridge, UK: Cambridge University Press.

Blockmans, W. and M. t'Hart (2013). "Power." In P. Clark, ed., *Oxford Handbook of Cities in World History*, pp. 421–37, Oxford, UK: Oxford University Press.

Bockstette, V., Chanda, A., and Putterman, L. (2002). "States and Markets: The Advantage of an Early Start." *Journal of Economic Growth*, 7: 347–69.

Boffa, F., A. Piolatti, and G. Ponzetto (2016). "Political Centralization and Government Accountability." *Quarterly Journal of Economics*, 131: 381–422.

Bogart, D. (2011). "Did the Glorious Revolution Contribute to the Transport Revolution? Evidence from Investment in Roads and Rivers." *Economic History Review*, 64: 1073–112.

Boix, C. (2011). "Democracy, Development, and the International System." *American Political Science Review*, 105: 809–28.

Boix, C. (2015). *Political Order and Inequality*. Cambridge, UK: Cambridge University Press.

Boix, C. and S. Stokes (2003). "Endogenous Democratization." *World Politics*, 55: 517–49.

Boone, M. (2013). "Medieval Europe." In P. Clark, ed., *Oxford Handbook of Cities in World History*, pp. 221–39, Oxford, UK: Oxford University Press.

Brewer, J. (1989). *The Sinews of Power*. New York, NY: Knopf.

Bueno de Mesquita, M., A. Smith, R. Siverson, and J. Morrow (2003). *The Logic of Political Survival*. Cambridge, MA: MIT Press.

Caramani, Daniele (2000). *Elections in Western Europe Since 1815*. New York, NY: Groves.

Cassidy, T., M. Dincecco, and M. Onorato (2017). "The Economic Legacy of Warfare: Evidence from European Regions." Working paper, University of Michigan.

Centeno, M. (1997). "Blood and Debt: War and Taxation in Nineteenth-Century Latin America." *American Journal of Sociology*, 102: 1565–605.

Centeno, M. (2002). *Blood and Debt*. University Park, PA: Pennsylvania State University Press.

Chapman, J. (2017). "The Contribution of Infrastructure Investment to Britain's Urban Mortality Decline, 1861–1900." Working paper, NYU Abu Dhabi.

Cheibub, J. (1998). "Political Regimes and the Extractive Capacity of Governments: Taxation in Democracies and Dictatorships." *World Politics*, 50: 349–76.

Collier, P., V. Elliot, H. Hegre, A. Hoeffler, M. Reynal-Querol, and N. Sambanis (2013). *Breaking the Conflict Trap*. Washington, DC: World Bank and Oxford University Press.

Cox, G. (2011). "War, Moral Hazard, and Ministerial Responsibility: England after the Glorious Revolution." *Journal of Economic History*, 71: 133–61.

Cox, G. (2016). *Marketing Sovereign Promises*. Cambridge, UK: Cambridge University Press.

Cox, G. (2017). "Political Institutions, Economic Liberty, and the Great Divergence." Forthcoming, *Journal of Economic History*.

De Long, B. and A. Shleifer (1993). "Princes and Merchants: European City Growth Before the Industrial Revolution." *Journal of Law and Economics*, 36: 671–702.

de Vries, J. (1984). *European Urbanization: 1500–1800*. Cambridge, MA: Harvard University Press.

Dell, M., N. Lane, and P. Querubin (2015). "State Capacity, Local Governance, and Economic Development in Vietnam." Working paper, Harvard University.

Depetris-Chauvin, E. (2014). "State History and Contemporary Conflict: Evidence from Sub-Saharan Africa." Working paper, Brown University.

Dincecco, M. (2009). "Fiscal Centralization, Limited Government, and Public Revenues in Europe, 1650–1913." *Journal of Economic History*, 69: 48–103.

Dincecco, M. (2010). "Fragmented Authority from Ancien Régime to Modernity: A Quantitative Analysis." *Journal of Institutional Economics*, 6: 305–28.

Dincecco, M. (2011). *Political Transformations and Public Finances.* Cambridge, UK: Cambridge University Press.

Dincecco, M. (2015). "The Rise of Effective States in Europe." *Journal of Economic History*, 75: 901–18.

Dincecco, M., G. Federico, and A. Vindigni (2011). "Warfare, Taxation, and Political Change: Evidence from the Italian Risorgimento." *Journal of Economic History*, 71: 887–914.

Dincecco, M. and M. Prado (2012). "Warfare, Fiscal Capacity, and Performance." *Journal of Economic Growth*, 17: 171–203.

Dincecco, M. and G. Katz (2016). "State Capacity and Long-Run Economic Performance." *Economic Journal*, 126: 189–218.

Dincecco M. and M. Onorato (2017). *From Warfare to Wealth.* Cambridge, UK: Cambridge University Press.

Downing, B. (1992). *The Military Revolution and Political Change.* Princeton, NJ: Princeton University Press.

Drelichman, M. and H.J. Voth (2014). *Lending to the Borrower from Hell.* Princeton, NJ: Princeton University Press.

Economist (2006). "Impunity Rules; Guatemala." *Economist*, November 18.

Edling, M. (2003). *A Revolution in Favor of Government.* Oxford, UK: Oxford University Press.

Evans, P. (1995). *Embedded Autonomy.* Princeton, NJ: Princeton University Press.

Epstein, S. (2000). *Freedom and Growth.* London, UK: Routledge.

Ertman, T. (1997). *Birth of the Leviathan.* Cambridge, UK: Cambridge University Press.

Fenske, J. (2013). "Does Land Abundance Explain African Institutions?" *Economic Journal*, 123: 1363–90.

Fenske, J. and N. Kala (2017). "1807: Economic Shocks, Conflict, and the Slave Trade." *Journal of Development Economics*, 126: 66–76.

Flora, Peter, 1983. *State, Economy, and Society in Western Europe: 1815–1975*. London, UK: St. James Press.

Ferejohn, J. and F. Rosenbluth, G. (2010). "War and State Building in Medieval Japan." In J. Ferejohn and F. Rosenbluth, eds., *War and State Building in Medieval Japan*, pp. 1–20, Palo Alto, CA: Stanford University Press.

Frankema, E. and M. van Waijenburg (2014). "Metropolitan Blueprints of Colonial Taxation? Lessons from Fiscal Capacity Building in British and French Africa, 1880-1940." *Journal of African History*, 55: 371–400.

Fukuyama, F. (2004). "The Imperative of State-Building." *Journal of Democracy*, 15: 17–31.

Fukuyama, F. (2011). *The Origins of Political Order*. New York, NY: Farrar, Straus and Giroux.

Feenstra, R., R. Inklaar, and M. Timmer (2015), "The Next Generation of the Penn World Table." *American Economic Review*, 105: 3150–82.

Galor, O. and O. Moav (2004). "From Physical to Human Capital Accumulation: Inequality and the Process of Development." *Review of Economic Studies*, 71: 1001–26.

Ganshof, F. (1971). "On the Genesis and Significance of the Treaty of Verdun (843)." In F. Ganshof, ed., *The Carolingians and the Frankish Monarchy*, pp. 289–302, Ithaca, NY: Cornell University Press.

García-Ponce, O. and L. Wantchekon (2015) "Critical Junctures: Independence Movements and Democracy in Africa." Working paper, Princeton University.

Garfias, F. (2016). "Elite Coalitions, Limited Government, and Fiscal Capacity Development: Evidence from Bourbon Mexico." Working paper, University of California, San Diego.

Gardner, L. (2012). *Taxing Colonial Africa*. Oxford, UK: Oxford University Press.

Gelderblom, O. and J. Jonker (2011). "Public Finance and Economic Growth: The Case of Holland in the Seventeenth Century." *Journal of Economic History*, 71: 1–39.

Gennaioli, N. and I. Rainer (2007). "The Modern Impact of Pre-Colonial Centralization in Africa." *Journal of Economic Growth*, 12: 185-234.

Gennaioli, N., R. La Porta, F. Lopez-de-Silanes, and A. Shleifer (2013). "Human Capital and Regional Development." *Quarterly Journal of Economics*, 128: 105–64.

Gennaioli, N. and H.J. Voth (2015). "State Capacity and Military Conflict." *Review of Economic Studies*, 82: 1409–48.

Glaeser, E. (2016). "If You Build It . . . Myths and Realities About America's Infrastructure Spending." *City Journal*, Summer.

Glaeser, E., R. La Porta, F. Lopez-De-Silanes, and A. Shleifer (2004). "Do Institutions Cause Growth?" *Journal of Economic Growth*, 9: 271–303.

Grafe, R. and A. Irigoin (2006). "The Spanish Empire and Its Legacy: Fiscal Redistribution and Political Conflict in Colonial and Post-Colonial Spanish America." *Journal of Global History*, 1: 241–67.

Greif, A. (1993). "Contract Enforceability and Economic Institutions in Early Trade: The Maghribi Traders' Coalition." *American Economic Review*, 83: 525–48.

Greif, A. and M. Iyigun (2013). "Social Organizations, Violence, and Modern Growth." *American Economic Review: Papers and Proceedings*, 103: 534–8.

Guinnane, T. and J. Streb (2011). "Moral Hazard in a Mutual Health Insurance System: German Knappschaften, 1867–1914." *Journal of Economic History*, 71: 70–104.

Gupta, B., D. Ma, and T. Roy (2016). "States and Development: Early Modern India, China, and the Great Divergence." In J. Eloranta, E. Golson, E. Markevich, and N. Wolf, eds., *Economic History of Warfare and State Formation*, pp. 51–69, Berlin, Germany: Springer.

Hale, J. (1985). *War and Society in Renaissance Europe, 1450–1620*. Baltimore, MD: Johns Hopkins University Press.

Hall, R. and C. Jones (1999). "Why do Some Countries Produce So Much More Output per Worker than Others?" *Quarterly Journal of Economics*, 114: 83–116.

Hanson, J. (2014). "Forging then Taming Leviathan: State Capacity, Constraints on Rulers, and Development." *International Studies Quarterly*, 58: 380–92.

Herbst, J. (2000). *States and Power in Africa*. Princeton, NJ: Princeton University Press.

Hoffman, P. (2015a). "What Do States Do? Politics and Economic History." *Journal of Economic History*, 75: 303–32.

Hoffman, P. (2015b). *Why Did Europe Conquer the World?* Princeton, NJ: Princeton University Press.

Hoffman, P. and J.L. Rosenthal (1997). "The Political Economy of Warfare and Taxation in Early Modern Europe: Historical Lessons for Economic

Development." In J. Drobak and J. Nye, eds., *The Frontiers of the New Institutional Economics*, pp. 31–55, St. Louis, MO: Academic Press.

Hui, V. (2005). *War and State Formation in Ancient China and Early Modern Europe*. Cambridge, UK: Cambridge University Press.

Huillery, E. (2014). "The Black Man's Burden: The Cost of Colonization of French West Africa." *Journal of Economic History*, 74: 1–38.

Huntington, S. (1968). *Political Order in Changing Societies*. New Haven, CT: Yale University Press.

IMF World Revenue Longitudinal Database. http://data.imf.org.

International Country Risk Guide. http://epub.prsgroup.com.

Johnson, C. (1982). *MITI and the Japanese Miracle*. Palo Alto, CA: Stanford University Press.

Johnson, N. (2006). "Banking on the King: The Evolution of the Royal Revenue Farms in Old Regime France." *Journal of Economic History*, 66: 963–91.

Johnson, N. and M. Koyama (2014). "Tax Farming and the Origins of State Capacity in England and France." *Explorations in Economic History*, 51: 1–20.

Karaman, K. and Ş. Pamuk (2010). "Ottoman State Finances in European Perspective, 1500–1914." *Journal of Economic History*, 70: 593–629.

Karaman, K. and Ş. Pamuk (2013). "Different Paths to the Modern State in Europe: The Interaction Between Domestic Political Economy and Interstate Competition." *American Political Science Review*, 107: 603–26.

Kesztenbaum, L. and J.L. Rosenthal (2017). "Sewers' Diffusion and the Decline of Mortality: The Case of Paris, 1880–1914." *Journal of Urban Economics*, 98: 174–86.

Kiser, E. and Y. Cai (2003). "War and Bureaucratization in Qin China: Exploring an Anomalous Case." *American Sociological Review*, 68: 511–39.

Ko, C.Y., M. Koyama, and T.H. Sng (2014). "Unified China and Divided Europe." Forthcoming, *International Economic Review*.

Koyama, M. and N. Johnson (2017). "States and Economic Growth: Capacity and Constraints." *Explorations in Economic History*, 64: 1–20.

Kurtz, M. (2013). *Latin American State Building in Comparative Perspective*. Cambridge, UK: Cambridge University Press.

Lazear, E. and S. Rosen (1981). "Rank-Order Tournaments as Optimum Labor Contracts." *Journal of Political Economy*, 89: 841–64.

Levi M. (1988). *Of Rule and Revenue*. Berkeley, CA: University of California Press.

Lipset, S. (1959). "Some Social Requisites of Democracy: Economic Development and Political Legitimacy." *American Political Science Review*, 53: 69–105.

Lindert, P. (2004). *Growing Public*. Cambridge, UK: Cambridge University Press.

Liu, W. (2015). "The Making of a Fiscal State in Song China, 960–1279." *Economic History Review*, 68: 48–78.

Lizzeri, A. and Persico, N. (2004). "Why Did the Elites Extend the Suffrage? Democracy and the Scope of Government, with an Application to Britain's 'Age of Reform.'" *Quarterly Journal of Economics*, 119: 707–65.

Lu, Y., M. Luan, and T.H. Sng (2016). "The Effect of State Capacity Under Different Economic Systems." Working paper, National University of Singapore.

Lucas, R. (1988). "On the Mechanics of Economic Development." *Journal of Monetary Economics*, 22: 3–42.

Ma, D. and J. Rubin (2016). "The Paradox of Power: Understanding Fiscal Capacity in Imperial China." Working paper, London School of Economics.

Madison, J. (1788). "Federalist #51." In L. Goldman, ed., *The Federalist Papers* [2008], pp. 256–60, Oxford, UK: Oxford University Press.

Maddison Project (2013). www.ggdc.net/maddison/maddison-project /home.htm.

Mann, M. (1986). "The Autonomous Power of the State: Its Origins, Mechanisms, and Results." In J. Hall, ed., *States in History*, pp. 109–36, Oxford, UK: Oxford University Press.

Mares, I. and D. Queralt (2015). "The Non-Democratic Origins of Income Taxation." *Comparative Political Studies*, 48: 1974–2009.

Michalopoulos, S. and E. Papaioannou (2013). "Pre-Colonial Ethnic Institutions and Contemporary African Development." *Econometrica*, 81: 113–52.

Milanovic, B. (2016). "Income Inequality is Cyclical." *Nature*, 537: 479–82.

Mokyr, J. (1998). "The Second Industrial Revolution, 1870–1914." In Valerio Castronovo, ed., *Storia dell'economia Mondiale*, Rome, Italy: Laterza.

Mokyr, J. (1995). "Urbanization, Technological Progress, and Economic History." In H. Giersch, ed., *Urban Agglomeration and Economic Growth*, pp. 3–38, Berlin, Germany: Springer.

Mokyr, J. (2009). *The Enlightened Economy.* New Haven, CT: Yale University Press.

Moscona, J., N. Nunn, and J. Robinson (2017). "Keeping It in the Family: Lineage Organization and the Scope of Trust in Sub-Saharan Africa." *American Economic Review: Papers and Proceedings*, 107: 565–71.

Musacchio, A. and S. Lazzarini (2014). *Reinventing State Capitalism.* Cambridge, MA: Harvard University Press.

New York Times (2014). "Afghan Army's Test Begins with Fight for Vital Highway." February 15.

New York Times (2016). "How the Most Dangerous Place on Earth Got Safer." August 11.

New York Times (2016). "Poverty, Drought, and Felled Trees Imperil Malawi Water Supply." August 20.

Nafziger, S. (2011). "Did Ivan's Vote Matter? The Case of the Zemstvo in Tsarist Russia." *European Review of Economic History*, 15: 393–441.

North, D. (1981). *Structure and Change in Economic History.* New York, NY: Norton.

North, D. (1990). *Institutions, Institutional Change, and Economic Performance.* Cambridge, UK: Cambridge University Press.

North, D. and R. Thomas (1973). *The Rise of the Western World.* Cambridge, UK: Cambridge University Press.

North, D. and B. Weingast (1989). "Constitutions and Commitment: The Evolution of Institutions Governing Public Choice in Seventeenth-Century England." *Journal of Economic History*, 49: 803–32.

North, D., J. Wallis, and B. Weingast (2009). *Violence and Social Orders.* Cambridge, UK: Cambridge University Press.

Nunn, N. (2008). "The Long-Term Effects of Africa's Slaves Trades." *Quarterly Journal of Economics*, 123: 139–76.

Nunn, N. (2009). "The Important of History for Economic Development." *Annual Review of Economics*, 1: 65–92.

Nunn, N. and L. Wantchekon (2011). "The Slave Trade and the Origins of Mistrust in Africa." *American Economic Review*, 101: 3221–52.

Nye, J. (2007). *War, Wine, and Taxes.* Princeton, NJ: Princeton University Press.

O'Brien, P. (2011). "The Nature and Historical Evolution of an Exceptional Fiscal State and Its Possible Significant for the Precocious Commercialization and Industrialization of the British Economy from Cromwell to Nelson." *Economic History Review*, 64: 408–46.

O'Brien, P. (2012). "Afterword." In B. Yun-Casalilla, P. O'Brien, and F. Comín Comín, *The Rise of Fiscal States*, pp. 442–53, Cambridge, UK: Cambridge University Press.

Oates, W. (1999). "An Essay on Fiscal Federalism." *Journal of Economic Literature*, 37: 1120–49.

Okun, A. (2015). *Equality and Efficiency*. Washington, DC: Brookings Institution Press.

Olson, M. (1965). *The Logic of Collective Action*. Cambridge, MA: Harvard University Press.

Osafo-Kwaako, P. and J. Robinson (2013). "Political Centralization in Pre-Colonial Africa." *Journal of Comparative Economics*, 41: 6–21.

Ostrom, E. (1990). *Governing the Commons*. Cambridge, UK: Cambridge University Press.

Ostry, J., A. Berg, and C. Tsangarides (2014). "Redistribution, Inequality, and Growth." IMF working paper SDN/14/02.

Papaioannou, E. and G. Siourounis (2008). "Democratisation and Growth." *Economic Journal*, 118: 1520–51.

Parker, G. (1996). *The Military Revolution*. Cambridge, UK: Cambridge University Press.

Pepinsky, T. (2016). "Colonial Migration and the Deep Origins of Governance: Theory and Evidence from Java." *Comparative Political Studies*, 49: 1201–37.

Piketty, T. (2014). *Capital in the Twenty-First Century*. Cambridge, MA: Harvard University Press.

Pincus, S. and J. Robinson (2014). "What Really Happened During the Glorious Revolution?" In S. Galiani and I. Sened, eds., *Institutions, Property Rights, and Economic Growth*, pp. 192–222, Cambridge, UK: Cambridge University Press.

Pinker, S. (2011). *The Better Angels of Our Nature*. New York, NY: Penguin.

Prescott, E. (2004). "Why Do Americans Work So Much More than Europeans?" *Federal Reserve Bank of Minneapolis Quarterly Review*, 28: 2–13.

Przeworski, A., M. Alvarez, J. Cheibub, and F. Limongi (2000). *Democracy and Development*. Cambridge, UK: Cambridge University Press.

Przeworski, A., A., Tamar, and B. Thomas (2012). "The Origins of Parliamentary Responsibility." In T. Ginsburg, ed., *Comparative Constitutional Design*, pp. 101–37, Cambridge, UK: Cambridge University Press.

Queralt, D. (2015). "From Mercantilism to Free Trade: A History of Fiscal Capacity Building." *Quarterly Journal of Political Science*, 2015: 221–73.

Redding S. and M. Turner (2015). "Transportation Costs and the Spatial Organization of Economic Activity." In G. Duranton, V. Henderson, and W. Strange, eds., *Handbook of Regional and Urban Economics* (Volume 5b), pp. 1339–98, Amsterdam, Netherlands: Elsevier.

Reid, R. (2012). *Warfare in African History*. Cambridge, UK: Cambridge University Press.

Reid, R. (2014). "The Fragile Revolution: Rethinking War and Development in Africa's Violent Nineteenth Century." In E. Akyeampong, R. Bates, N. Nunn, and J. Robinson, eds., *Africa's Development in Historical Perspective*, pp. 393–423, Cambridge, UK: Cambridge University Press.

Reuters (2016). "Honduras Fires Top Police Officials to Purge Criminal Links." April 29.

Rice, S. and S. Patrick (2008). "Index of State Weakness in the Developing World." Brookings Institution.

Rodrik, D. (1999). "Where Did All the Growth Go? External Shocks, Social Conflict, and Growth Collapses." *Journal of Economic Growth*, 4: 385–412.

Rokkan, S. (1975). "Dimensions of State Formation and Nation-Building: A Possible Paradigm for Research on Variations Within Europe." In C. Tilly, ed., *The Formation of National States in Western Europe*, pp. 562–600, Princeton, NJ: Princeton University Press.

Rosenthal, J.L. (1992). *The Fruits of Revolution*. Cambridge, UK: Cambridge University Press.

Rosenthal, J.L. and R.B. Wong (2011). *Before and Beyond Divergence*. Cambridge, MA: Harvard University Press.

Roy, T. (2013). "Rethinking the Origins of British India: State Formation and Military-Fiscal Undertakings in an Eighteenth-Century World Region." *Modern Asian Studies*, 47: 1125–56.

Rubin, J. (2017). *Rulers, Religion, and Riches*. Cambridge, UK: Cambridge University Press.

Scheidel, W. (2017). *The Great Leveler*. Princeton, NJ: Princeton University Press.

Scheve, K. and D. Stasavage (2010). "The Conscription of Wealth: Mass Warfare and the Demand for Progressive Taxation." *International Organization*, 64: 529–61.

Scheve, K. and D. Stasavage (2012). "Democracy, War, and Wealth: Lessons from Two Centuries of Inheritance Taxation." *American Political Science Review*, 107: 81–102.

Scheve, K. and D. Stasavage (2016). *Taxing the Rich*. Princeton, NJ: Princeton University Press.

Slater, D. (2010). *Ordering Power*. Cambridge, UK: Cambridge University Press.

Smith, A. (2007). *An Inquiry into the Nature and Causes of the Wealth of Nations*. Amsterdam, Netherlands: Metalibri Digital Library.

Sng, T.H. and C. Moriguchi (2014). "Asia's Little Divergence: State Capacity in China and Japan before 1850." *Journal of Economic Growth*, 19: 439–70.

Soifer, H. (2015). *State Building in Latin America*. Cambridge, UK: Cambridge University Press.

Solow, R. (1956). "A Contribution to the Theory of Economic Growth." *Quarterly Journal of Economics*, 70: 65–94.

Stasavage, D. (2003). *Public Debt and the Birth of the Democratic State*. Cambridge, UK: Cambridge University Press.

Stasavage, D. (2011). *States of Credit*. Princeton, NJ: Princeton University Press.

Stasavage, D. (2014). "Was Weber Right? City Autonomy, Political Oligarchy, and the Rise of Europe." *American Political Science Review*, 108: 337–54.

Stasavage (2016a). "What We Can Learn from the Early History of Sovereign Debt." *Explorations in Economic History*, 59: 1–16.

Stasavage, D. (2016b). "Representation and Consent: Why They Arose in Europe and Not Elsewhere." *Annual Review of Political Science*, 19: 145–62.

Strayer, J. (1970). *On the Medieval Origins of the Modern State*. Princeton, NJ: Princeton University Press.

Summerhill, W. (2015). *Inglorious Revolution*. New Haven, CT: Yale University Press.

Thies, C. (2005). "War, Rivalry, and State-Building in Latin America." *American Journal of Political Science*, 49: 451–65.

Thies, C. (2007). "The Political Economy of State-Building in Sub-Saharan Africa." *Journal of Politics*, 69: 716–31.

Thornton, J. (1999). *Warfare in Atlantic Africa, 1500–1800*. London, UK: Routledge.

Tilly, C. (1975). "Reflections on the History of European State-Making." In C. Tilly, ed., *The Formation of States in Western Europe*, pp. 3–83, Princeton, NJ: Princeton University Press.

Tilly, C. (1992). *Coercion, Capital, and European States, 990–1992*. Cambridge, MA: Blackwell.

Timmons, J. (2005). "The Fiscal Contract: States, Taxes, and Public Services." *World Politics*, 57: 530–67.

Treisman, D. (2007). *The Architecture of Government*. Cambridge, UK: Cambridge University Press.

United Nations (2014). "Global Study on Homicide 2013." Vienna, Austria: United Nations Office on Drugs and Crime.

van Zanden, J.L. (2009). *The Long Road to the Industrial Revolution*. Leiden, Netherlands: Brill.

van Zanden, J.L., M. Bosker, and E. Buringh (2012). "The Rise and Decline of European Parliaments, 1188–1789." *Economic History Review*, 65: 835–61.

Verhulst, A. (1999). *The Rise of Cities in Northwest Europe*. Cambridge, UK: Cambridge University Press.

Wade, R. (1990). *Governing the Market*. Princeton, NJ: Princeton University Press.

Weber, M. (1946). *Essays in Sociology*. Oxford, UK: Oxford University Press.

Weber, M. (1958). *The City*. New York, NY: Free Press.

Weingast, B. (1995). "The Economic Role of Political Institutions: Market-Preserving Federalism and Economic Development." *Journal of Law, Economics, and Organization*, 11: 1–31.

Whatley, W. and R. Gillezeau (2011). "The Impact of the Transatlantic Slave Trade on Ethnic Stratification in Africa." *American Economic Review: Papers and Proceedings*, 101: 571–76.

White, E. (2001). "France and the Failure to Modernize Macroeconomic Institutions." In M. Bordo and R. Cortès-Conde, eds., *Transferring Wealth and Power from the Old to the New World*, pp. 59–99, Cambridge, UK: Cambridge University Press.

Woolf, S. (1991). *Napoleon's Integration of Europe*. London, UK: Routledge.

World Bank Doing Business Database. www.doingbusiness.org/.

World Top Incomes Database. http://wid.world/data/.

Zhu, X. (2012). "Understanding China's Growth: Past, Present, and Future." *Journal of Economic Perspectives*, 26: 103–24.

Printed in the United States
By Bookmasters